ECONOMICS
A Concise Introduction

G. A. MOHR, PHD
WORLD HONS MULT

ECONOMICS
A Concise Introduction

G. A. Mohr, PhD
World hons mult.

© G. A. Mohr, 2019

All rights reserved. No part of this publication may be reproduced, stored in a retrieval system, or transmitted in any form or by any means, electronic, mechanical, photocopying, recording, or otherwise, without the prior written permission of both the author and publisher.

G. A. Mohr
ECONOMICS: A Concise Introduction

TRI

Transworld Research & Innovation
9 Hampstead Drive
Hoppers Crossing VIC 3029
AUSTRALIA

Also by G. A. Mohr

Finite Elements for Solids, Fluids, and Optimization

A Microcomputer Introduction to the Finite Element Method

The Pretentious Persuaders,
A Brief History & Science of Mass Persuasion

Curing Cancer & Heart Disease,
Proven Ways to Combat Aging, Atherosclerosis & Cancer

The Variant Virus: Introducing Secret Agent Simon Sinclair

The Doomsday Calculation: The End Of The Human Race

The War of the Sexes, Women Are Getting On Top

Heart Disease, Cancer, & Ageing:
Proven Neutraceutical & Lifestyle Solutions

2045: A Remote Town Survives Global Holocaust

The History & Psychology of Human Conflict

Elementary Thinking for Modern Management

The 8-Week+ Program to Reverse Cardiovascular Disease

The Scientific MBA;   Mohr's Law of Hierarchies

The DIY Cardiovascular Cure,
A Comprehensive Program to Reverse Atherosclerosis

Combating Cancer: Proven Neutraceutical & Lifestyle Remedies

The Psychology of Life;   The Psychology of Depression

The Bullying Epidemic;   New Ideas for the 21st Century

With R.S. Mohr/Richard Sinclair & P.E. Mohr/Edwin Fear

The Evolving Universe: Relativity, Redshift and Life from Space

World Religions: The History, Psychology, Issues & Truth

The Population Explosion;   World War 3: When & How Will It End?

The Brainwashed: From Consumer Zombies to Islamic Jihad

Human Intelligence, Learning & Behaviour

New Theories of The Universe, Evolution, and Relativity

World Religions: From to Animism to Mohronism

Human Conflict: An Attitudinal Psychology Model

The Psychology of Hope;   The Psychology of Success

Human Psychology, Learning & Intelligence

Real Democracy;   DIY Psychology & Psychotherapy

ECONOMICS
A Concise Introduction

TABLE OF CONTENTS

Preface	1
1. Business Finance	3
2. International Economics	57
3. Microeconomics	93
4. Time Stepping Economic Models	133
5. The LMS and ISE Curves	137
6. Input Output Analysis	147
7. Supply and Demand Inverted	163
8. Globalization	169
9. Current Issues	177
10. Key Policy Objectives	187
11. Conclusions	195
Appendix: Introduction to BASIC	197

Preface

> *Let us assume we have a can opener.*
> *This was the response of the group of economists*
> *stranded on a desert island grappling with the task*
> *of opening the few cans of food that had washed ashore*
> *(in the days before ring-pull openers).*
> *My guess is that the implied pointlessness of economists in that*
> *joke is an opinion shared by many members of the public.*
> Judith Sloan, contributing economics editor,
> 'Are economists useful? A question to tax the brain.'
> *The Weekend Australian,* Nov. 21-22, 2015.

The present book is intended as a concise introduction to modern economics. It begins with comprehensive chapters on:

1. Business Finance.

2. International Economics (macroeconomic).

3. Microeconomics (national economics).

These are followed by chapters on economic models and methodologies that are new, or not found in most books on economics:

4. Time stepping models of national economies.

5. The Liquid Money Supply (LMS) and Interest Sensitive Expenditure (ISE) curves, using the equations for these to show that increasing official interest rates increase inflation, as intuition suggests.

6. Input-output analysis, a matrix model of the business sector.

Preface

7. An 'inverted' supply and demand model that applies better to manufactured products (the original model applying to commodities).

8. Globalization, a growing trend in recent decades, and now an important issue, as shown by the recent 'tariff war' between the USA and China.

9. Discussion of other important current issues in global trade, economics and politics.

10. Discussion of some of the key policy objectives that should be considered by governments around the world.

Use of the LMS and ISE curves to demonstrate that increasing interest rates *increases* inflation, and the inverted law of supply and demand for mass produced/manufactured products, represent important corrections of the views and practices of most of today's economists.

The book includes a few programs in QBASIC or Visual Basic so that, after the concluding chapter, an appendix on BASIC programming is included.

I hope that such topics as proof that increasing interest rates increases inflation, and my 'inverted' supply and demand model, prove both interesting and useful to many readers.

Finally, once again I am grateful to the publishers for yet again doing an excellent job of promptly publishing this book.

Geoff Mohr
Melbourne, 2019

Chapter 1

Business Finance (BF)

> *The farmer is the only man in our economy*
> *who buys everything retail, sells everything wholesale,*
> *and pays the freight both ways.*
> John F. Kennedy,
> campaign speech in Sioux Falls, South Dakota, Sep. 22, 1960.

Business finance involves important decisions such as, for example, whether to seek funding through *equity* (by issuing shares) or through *debt* (by borrowing from banks etc.), and good management requires a sound knowledge of 'BF'.

In practice some knowledge of accounting is also required and this is briefly introduced.

BF1. Introduction

Business finance involves several different types of activity which, though related, will often be carried out by different personnel or departments of a company. These include:

1. *Financial management.* This occurs at executive level and involves decisions on when and how to obtain finance, how to dispose of profits and on adjustments to company operations to improve profitability.

2. *Managerial accounting.* This is usually done at senior management level and involves 'overview accounting' of the company operations to provide the board and members (for example at the AGM) with information upon which to base financial management decisions.

3. *Departmental accounting.* This involves only the productivity, sales, inventory etc. figures and periodic control of these. At this level such matters as finance and taxation are not considered.

1. Business Finance

Sometimes there might be a further lower level dealing with 'over the counter' operations and day to day operations at this level. Such 'front line' data is passed up to (3), which in turn reports to (2), and so on.

Discussion of (1) commences in Sec. BF2 and examples of (2) can be found in BF4.

Often, of course, accounting is not done in house. Taxation accounting, for example, is an important specialty beyond the scope of the present text. Moreover, tax matters vary considerably between countries, of course, and even in a given country a very up to date knowledge of current taxation requirements is important and cannot be given in an overview text such as the present one.

Accounting software

Massive amounts of software are now available for PCs, principal accounting applications including:

[1] Spreadsheets

The impact of the computer has been considerable and spreadsheets for cash flow, accounts receivable, financial statements (of assets and liabilities), profit and loss accounts and balance sheets are much used and changes in figures at any point in a large accounting system are instantly transferred throughout the system.

Many financial functions are available, along with 'math' options such as *regression, what-if?, distribution* and *automatic graphing* (the reader should try these) and some programs (e.g. Quattro) include optimization of both linear and non-linear problems.

[2] Databases

Databases, of course, are primarily intended for storing and retrieving data and consequently require such features as efficient searching and sorting routines. Common applications relating to accounting involve long term storage of company accounts and storage of customer information files (including address for invoicing, accounts owing etc.).

1. BUSINESS FINANCE

[3] Statistical analysis packages

The most common of these are for analysis of variations in share, currency and commodity prices etc. In the case of players on the currency market, for example, decisions must be made very quickly (literally 'before breakfast') and software for this is often developed in house by private and government organizations interested in currency matters.

Applications of accounting via PCs, of course, also include packages for personal or household budgeting. At the other end of the spectrum, package programs for large computer networks are now widely used.

Introduction to financial mathematics

Simple interest

For this the *accumulated value* is given by $S = P(1 + ni)$ where P is the *principal*, I is the interest rate and n is the number of periods (usually years).

Then the *present value* of a sum (S) n years hence is
$PV = S/(1 + ni)$.

Compound interest

(BF1) $S = P(1 + i)^n$
(BF2) $PV = S/(1 + i)^n$

Annuities

For these S accumulates via a *geometric progression*:
(BF3) $S = a + ar + ar^2 + \cdots\cdots + ar^{n-1}$ where $r = 1 + i$

giving $Sr = ar + ar^2 + \cdots\cdots + ar^{n-1} + ar^n$

when Eqn BF3 is multiplied by r.

Subtracting Equation BF3 from this result we obtain
(BF4) $S = a(r^n - 1)/(r - 1)$

(BF5) and $PV = S/r^n = a(1 - 1/r^n)/(r - 1) = a/(r - 1)$
$n \to \infty$, $r > 1$

the last result being for a *perpetual annuity*.

1. BUSINESS FINANCE

Example: As an example of the latter, suppose a philanthropist wishes to give a scholarship of *$1000* p.a. How much capital is needed at $i = 8\%$?
The answer is given by $PV = a/(r - 1) = 1000/0.08 = \$12{,}500$.

General annuities. These involve such variations as interest (at a *nominal rate i*) compounded m times per year and payments made monthly. Two common examples are:

[1] The compounding period is made equal to the payment period, when an *effective* rate of j is calculated using

$$1 + j = (1 + i/m)^m$$

Then if $i = 5\%$ we obtain $j = 5.0945\%$ for $m = 4$ and $j = 5.1162\%$ for $m = 12$.

[2] The payment period is made equal to the compounding period when an *equivalent 'a'* is calculated using
$$a' = a(r^{n'} - 1)/(r - 1) \text{ where } n' = m/p$$

where m = no. of interest payments per year and p = no. of annuity payments per year.

Continuous compounding

This corresponds to interest being calculated m times per year where m approaches infinity. Then to calculate the effective rate of interest we write

$$1 + j = (1 + i/m)^m \to e^i \text{ as } m \to \infty$$

giving $\quad j = e^i - 1 = 2.71829^i - 1$

For example, when $i = 6\%$ (0.06) we obtain $j = 6.18365\%$.

Conclusion

Awareness of effective interest rates has every day application whilst Equation BF2 is much used in calculating net present value of project proposals, in turn allowing the comparison of alternative schemes (see BF3).

BF2. Introduction to financial management

Financial management

Financial management involves such activities as
a. Raising capital (for example to acquire assets).
b. Setting the mix of debt and equity capital.
c. Studying alternative investment options.
d. Decisions on payment of dividends or reinvestment.
e. Valuing assets, liabilities, shares etc.
f. Decisions on amalgamations, takeovers etc.

Information required for such purposes includes knowledge of:
1. Company objectives and strategies.
2. Accounting procedures and economics.
3. Analytical models such as the Capital Asset Pricing Model (CAPM).
4. The financial environment, that is economic trends, institutional (banks, government etc.) trends, legal restrictions, competitors and markets.

The role of the CFO

The role of the chief financial officer is to:

1. Maximize the value of the company by maximizing cash flow and balancing debt and equity (the optimum balance is called the *optimal capital structure (OCS)*).
2. Deal with the CEO, company planners (including the board), the MDs (for MR, HRM etc.) and other interested parties within the company.
3. Deal with banks, trusts, shareholders, stock brokers, market analysts etc.
4. Facilitate company growth by appropriate choices, timing etc.
5. Form financial strategy consistent with company objectives and management, shareholders etc. wishes and targets.
6. Set financial targets (both short and long term)

1. BUSINESS FINANCE

Analysing financial decisions

[1] *Investment decisions:*   (a) A or B ?
                                     (b) fits BP ?
                                     (c) return on capital (ROC) ?

[2] *Capital management decisions:*
                     (a) for operations.
                     (b) for investments.
                     (c) how much finance needed ?
                     (d) when needed ?

[3] *Financing decisions:* from cash flow, equity, debt ?

Cost of capital

In financial management the costs of various sources of capital are of crucial importance in decision making. Also of importance is the *weighted average cost of capital (WACC)* of a company and this is calculated as follows:

(BF6) $WACC = k_0 = k_e(E/V) + k_d(1 - t_c)(D/V)$

where k_e = WAC of equity, k_d = WAC of debt
               E = monetary value of the company's equity
               D = monetary value of the company's debt
               $V = E + D$ = 'MV' of total capital
               t_c = company tax rate

Then the *leverage* of the company is the ratio of D to the net worth of the company, whilst the OCS (optimal capital structure) is the optimum value of E/D.

When there are several debt sources these are summed in Equation BF6, that is we use

$$\Sigma \, (k_d)_i \, (1 - t_c)(D_i/V)$$

and likewise when there are various sources of equity capital (for example preferential shares, ordinary shares etc.).

1. BUSINESS FINANCE

The following table gives an example of calculation of WACC.

(1) Source	(2) $(k)	(3) Proportion %	(4) Cost %	(5) WC = (3) x (4)
Bank O/D	200	10.26	7.10	0.728
Debentures	510	26.15	7.36	1.925
Pref. shares	190	9.74	13.68	1.332
Equity	1050	53.85	16.29	8.722
TOTAL	1950	100.00		12.707 = k_o

Interest rates

Some understanding of the behaviour of interest rates and the factors which lead to that behaviour is, of course, essential in financial management as such factors will also affect market conditions etc. Examples of how some logic can be seen in the behaviour of interest rates include the following:

[1] Historical trends in interest rates are important. For example Australian government 10 year bonds went from 3% in 1946 to 13% in 1986 with a peak of 16% along the way. From 13% in 1983, on the other hand, they went to 12% in 1988. Clearly, therefore, long term trends and short term ones are a very different matter.

[2] Factors affecting interest rates include:
a. *Demand* from the public sector, households etc.
b. *Supply* from savings, overseas funds etc.
c. Overseas rates (for example Australian rates are always higher but tend to follow the trends of US rates, but a little behind in time).
d. Balance of payments (current account).

[3] There is a process called the *transmission mechanism* whereby monetary policy affects interest rates etc., ultimately itself being affected by the results. This cycle has the following steps:
a. Government alters monetary policy.
b. Official cash rates affected.
c. Other short term rates affected.
d. General rates affected.
e. Demand for credit.
f. Spending alters (reduces/increases).
g. Inflation rates alter (up/down).
h. Back to (a).

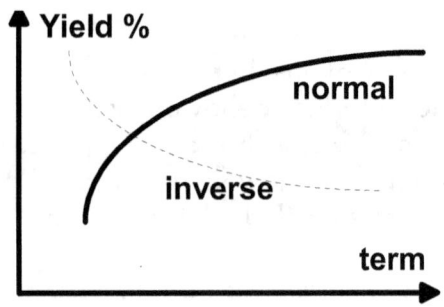

Fig BF1. Yield curves for interest rates

[4] The *yield curve* for interest rates of various terms (durations) of lending is usually upward sloping, as shown in Figure BF1.

Such upward sloping curves are *normal*. *Inverse* yield curves can occur, however, for example when there is strong expectation of a fall in official rates. When such expectation is of a rise, on the other hand, normal curves may become stronger.

Conclusion

In the foregoing introductory discussion of financial management and relevant matters three categories of financial decision were briefly discussed, namely investment, capital management and financing decisions. Each of these is considered in detail in the three sections that follow.

BF3. Investment decisions

Investment decisions (capital budgeting) are based on such considerations as:

Strategic fit. Is the decision in line with business policy?

Economic return. Is the return on capital (ROC) greater than the capital cost? Here we define ROC as the cash flow from a project over its life span converted to present value. The present value calculation requires use of an appropriate *discount rate* such as the weighted average cost of capital (WACC).

OCS. Is the decision consistent with achieving/maintaining an *optimal capital structure* (the optimum proportions of debt and equity). Here considerations such as the greater tax deductions but also greater business risk associated with debt capital.

Generally it is advisable to base the company capital structures on that of similar companies ('twin companies'). Public utilities, for example, tend to have high debt which they can support because of their 'guaranteed' market whereas companies with highly variable/uncertain sales tend to have high equity.

Capital asset pricing model

In Section BF2 k_0 or the WACC is given by

$$k_o = \% \text{ LT debt} \times k_d + \% \text{ equity} \times k_e$$

where k_d and k_e are respectively the weighted average costs of debt and equity. For example, when a company holds half its debt at two rates, 10 and 12%, and the company tax rate is 48% we obtain

(BF7) $k_d' = k_d (1 - t_c) = (10\% \times 0.5 + 12\% \times 0.5)(1 - 0.48) = 5.7\%$

In the *capital asset pricing model (CAPM)* the cost of equity is given by

(BF8) $k_e = R(f) + \beta [R(m) - R(f)]$

where

$R(f)$ is the *risk free* rate for bonds etc. and this is approximately the inflation rate multiplied by a factor such as $x = 1.2$.

1. Business Finance

$R(m)$ is the *market rate*, that is the rate for market stock such as those of the top 100 companies (not atypical companies, of course).

β is the *risk factor* which = 1 for companies with average risk, is < 1 for 'safe' companies and, for example, » 2 for volatile stock.

For example, if $R(f)$ = 8% and $R(m)$ = 10 to 12% (use the higher figure) and β = 1.2 (a not uncommon value) then

$$k_e = 8\% + 1.2(12 - 8) = 12.8\%$$

so that if k_d' is as calculated in Eqn BP7 we obtain the WACC as

(BF9) $k_0 = 5.7 \times 0.5 + 12.8 \times 0.5 = 9.25\%$

if debt = equity = 50% of capital.

Discounted cash flow analysis

Discounted cash flow analysis (DCF) is one of the principal tools for investment decisions. It involves calculating the net present value (NPV) of a project as the present value of the sum of the projected cash flows minus the initial project cost.

For example, if we have $4,000 to invest and the estimated net annual cash flows which will result from two alternative projects are:

Project	year 1	year 2	year 3	year 4
A	-4,000	2,000	2,000	0
B	-4,000	500	-500	6,000

Calculating the NPVs using the WACC obtained in Eqn BF9:

(BF10) NPV of A = $- C + \sum_{n=1}^{N} R_n /(1 + k)^n$
$$= - 4000 + 2000/1.0925 + 2000/1.0925^2 + 0$$
$$= - 4000 + 1831 + 1676 + 0 = - 493$$
NPV of B = $- 4000 + 500/1.0925 - 500/1.0925^2 + 6000/1.0925^3$
$$= - 4000 + 458 - 419 + 4601 = 640$$

so that B is, though it may not have appeared so at first sight, in the longer term at least, the more profitable project.

1. BUSINESS FINANCE

Delegation process for DCF analysis

This is to first eliminate proposals that are not consistent with company strategy or BP. Then the NPVs of the remaining projects are compared to the initial outlays that they require and the preferred project(s) are chosen. If there is no project with a positive NPV result, however, then it may be decided to pay dividends, for example, rather than reinvest.

Valuing an acquisition

This involves the seller estimating a value = S and the (potential) buyer makes an (initial) estimate = B. Assuming $S > B$ then both estimates are adjusted until $(S - B)/B$ is sufficiently small when the buyer is finally prepared to buy. This states the obvious but it is important to consider the question of possible overvaluation of assets in both financial decision making and accounting.

Retirement decisions

The foregoing DCF analysis assumed a project period of $N = 4$ years. Some projects, however, are indefinite or up to some *retirement* date. For example, in the case of machinery with a salvage value S_N at retirement the NPV is given by

(BF11) $NPV = \sum R_n/(1 + k)^n - C + S_N/(1 + k)^N$

If, for example, the machinery is 6 years old and has an estimated life of another 2 years then the retirement decision can be based on the following data:

Retirement end year	6	7	8
Net cash inflow	-	8,000	5,000
Salvage value	12,000	6,000	0

Assuming $k = 10\%$ the NPVs are calculated as
$NPV(7) = -12000 + 8000/1.1 + 6000/1.1 = 727$
$NPV(8) = -12000 + 8000/1.1 + 5000/1.1^2 = -595$
so that retirement at the end of year 7 is the preferred option.

Replacement

If items need to be replaced, rather than retired, then we substitute $(S_N - C_N)$ where $C_N > S_N$ for S_N in Equation BP1, noting that here C_N is the capital replacement cost at year N which may differ from the initial cost C. Alternatively, where there is no salvage value, C_N must be subtracted from the cash flow for the year of replacement.

Projects with different lives

As an example, let A have a 1 year life and B a three year life. Then with replacement of A the NPVs for A and B are given by

Year	0	1	2	3	NPV
A (life = 1)	-20,000	24,000	0	0	1,818
B (life = 3)	-20,000	10,000	10,000	10,000	4,868
A (replace)	-20,000	-20,000 24,000	-20,000 24,000	- 24,000	4,976

Hence A (with replacement) is the preferred option. Note that B here has the same initial cost but much longer life with lesser resulting output or annual cash flow. This is based on the assumption that A is operated more intensely but, as a result, over a shorter period.

Capital rationing.

In practice available capital is limited and this limits project selection. Suppose, for example, that there are several alternative projects and we wish not only to establish which has the best NPV, but also to include as many as possible additional projects, but keeping within some capital limit or *constraint*. Then the following example illustrates alternative selection processes that may be used.

1. BUSINESS FINANCE

Project	A	B	C	D	E	F
C_i ($ 000)	200	200	200	200	400	400
NPV	28	20	15	35	45	23
NPV/C_i	0.14	0.1	0.07	0.17	0.11	0.05

The capital constraint is $\sum C_i \leq 600$ k ($)

By inspection we might choose projects A, B and D, giving a total NPV of 83k with total outlay of 600k, just satisfying the capital limit.

Comparing on the basis of NPV/C_i, however, we would choose project D first, then A and then E. The latter violates the capital limit, however, so that we make B the third choice instead. The same solution has been obtained, but with a little more conviction. In addition we have given priorities to the projects and are better positioned to alter our decision if, for example, the capital limit is changed.

The foregoing problem can be stated in the general form

(BF12)   Maximize $\sum NPV_i \, x_i$ $x_i = 0$ or 1 only

subject to the constraints: (i) $\sum C_i x_i \leq C_{lim}$ (ii) $x_A + x_B \leq 1$

where constraint (ii) stipulates that projects A and B are *mutually exclusive* and there may be other such constraints.

This is an *Integer Programming problem,* a special case of *linear programming,* a well-known technique for optimizing problems expressed in linear algebraic form.

Conclusion

In making investment decisions acronyms abound and WACC, OCS, CAPM and NPV are important tools. In particular DCF (discounted cash flow) analysis using NPVs is important in project selection and also may include such considerations as retirement and replacement and capital constraints.

1. BUSINESS FINANCE

BF4. Capital management decisions

When investment decisions have been made we know our capital requirements but next planning is needed to determine *when* capital is required. This is done by preparing *pro forma* income and balance sheets for the projected cash flow and capital requirements. In different companies this may be done anything from daily up to every few years to calculate the level of assets, expenses, debts etc. to be financed.

Pro forma statements

These take the form: Year 1   Year 2   Year 3   Year 4
sales - cost of goods sold
gross profit - operating expenses
earnings - interest expenses
profit before taxes - taxes
<u>profit after taxes - dividends</u>
change in retained earnings

Then the forecast change in retained earnings is included in a pro forma balance sheet which might look as follows:

                            Year 1   Year 2

Assets
cash   - estimate cash needs
accounts receivable   - estimate sales
inventory   - estimate stock
net fixed assets -present assets +projected capital expenditures
                         - depreciation - projected asset sales
other assets -e.g. secured patents, loans to affiliate companies
Total assets (a)
Liabilities and equity
accounts payable   - projected owing on inventory etc.
accrued expenses   - operating expenses
long-term debt   - present +/- projected repayments/new loans
shareholders' funds   - present + projected new issues
<u>retained earnings   </u>- from pro forma income statement
Total liabilities and equity (b)
Other funding required: (b) - (a) gives this.

1. BUSINESS FINANCE

Here the 'out of balance' projected for each year ((b) - (a)) is the amount of money required to finance all the company's planned activities (assuming (b) - (a) is positive - if not then profit disposal decisions are required).

Sensitivity analysis

The term *sensitivity analysis* refers to experimental changes in a system to gauge their effect. In the case of pro formas for projected cash flow and finance requirements, for example, it is useful to prepare both best and west case statements. Then if the worst case statement is still a viable proposition the associated plan of company activities can proceed with greater confidence.

Example accounts

Tables BF1 and BF2 give examples of (a) a balance sheet, (b) a profit and loss account and (c) a statement of financial position. These, of course, are more formal than those required for planning purposes only, as above.

Table BF1 (part 1).
Balance sheet as at June 30 1999

1998	Assets		1999
$	*Current assets*	$	$
10,000	Cash	10,000	
110,000	Marketable securities	150,000	
180,000	Net accounts receivable	200,000	
350,000	Inventories (at lower of cost or market)	340,000	
650,000	Total current assets		700,000
	Fixed assets		
1,500,000	Fixed assets	1,600,000	
350,000	*less* Accumulated depreciation	400,000	
1,150,000	Total fixed assets		1,200,000

1. BUSINESS FINANCE

	Liabilities		
	Current liabilities		
30,000	Bank overdraft	40,000	
50,000	Commercial bills	40,000	
130,000	Accounts payable	120,000	
<u>120,000</u>	Provision for taxes	<u>100,000</u>	
330,000	Total current liabilities		300,000
	Long term liabilities		
300,000	Debentures	400,000	
<u>150,000</u>	Mortgages	<u>100,000</u>	
<u>450,000</u>			<u>500,000</u>
	Total liabilities		
780,000			800,000
	Shareholders' funds		
1,000,000	2,000,000 ord. shares par value 50c		
			1,000,000
200,000	Issued and paid-up capital	200,000	
300,000	Share premium reserve	300,000	
120,000	General reserve	150,000	
<u>400,000</u>	Retained earnings	<u>450,000</u>	
<u>1,020,000</u>	Total shareholders' funds		<u>1,100,000</u>
<u>1,800,000</u>	Total liabilities+ shareholder's funds		<u>1,900,000</u>

Table BF1 (part 2). Profit & loss a/c - year ended 30/6/1999

1999			1998
$		$	$
3,100,000	Net sales		3,100,000
<u>2,640,000</u>	Less Cost of goods sold		<u>2,700,000</u>
460,000	Gross profit		400,000
	less operating expenses		
50,000	Selling	70,000	
50,000	Administration	60,000	
<u>60,000</u>	Finance (Interest)	<u>70,000</u>	
<u>160,000</u>	Total operating expenses		<u>200,000</u>
300,000	Operating profit (taxable income)		200,000
<u>150,000</u>	less Tax (at 50%)		<u>100,000</u>
<u>150,000</u>	Operating profit after tax		<u>100,000</u>

1. Business Finance

Table BF2. Statement of financial position for 'IBC'.

Statement of financial position as at 31 May 1999				
	Thousands of dollars $ 000			
	Consolidated		Parent company	
Funds provided	**1999**	1998	**1999**	1998
Shareholder's equity				
Paid up capital of IBC shareholders	**441,506**	441,506	**441,506**	441,506
Reserves & unappropriated profits	**1,567,237**	1,427,959	**719,694**	671,501
Total IBC shareholders' equity	2,008,743	1,869,465		
Shareholders equity in subsidiary co's	**39,013**	36,790		
Total shareholders' equity	**2,047,756**	1,906,255	**1,161,200**	683,319
Non-current liabilities	**951,439**	942,972	**693,041**	683,319
Current liabilities				
Provisions	**309,150**	304,187	**41,043**	48,523
Loans repayable within 12 months	**63,825**	33,855	**28,259**	23,395
Creditors	**230,558**	317,626	**156,051**	127,389
	603,533	655,668	**225,353**	199,307
Total funds provided	**3,602,728**	3,504,895	**2,079,594**	1,995,633
These funds are represented by				
Fixed assets	**2,110,868**	2,054,359	**581,363**	582,633
Investments	**273,600**	250,211	**856,138**	749,470
Other non-current assets	**28,202**	30,034	**25,801**	25,700
Current assets				
Inventories	**648,294**	619,792	**176,590**	183,356
Debtors	**228,762**	188,863	**217,148**	203,544
Net liquids	**233,201**	281,535	**222,554**	248,930
	1,110,257	1,090,190	**616,292**	637,830
Intangibles	**79,801**	80,101		
Total assets employed	**3,602,728**	3,504,895	**2,079,594**	1,995,633

1. BUSINESS FINANCE

BF5. Financing decisions

Having planned company activities (for example using DCF analysis to choose projects) and then determined the funding requirements of the company we must then decide how to raise this funding. At this point it is important to realize that funds can be generated internally as well as externally.

Internally generated funds

This involves careful asset and liability management. Means by which funds can thus be generated internally include:

a. Hasten accounts receivable collection (this involves the risk of disenchanting some customers).
b. Speed up production and inventory turnover.
c. By asset sales, for example of property or equipment.
d. Slow accounts payable settlement (this too involves a risk, such as banks foreclosing on loans, debenture holders applying for receivership etc.)
e. Extend the terms of bank loans.
f. Increase prices.
g. Reduce expenses.
h. Reduce or defer dividends.

The list could go on and some of the points are all too obvious but others may not be, indicating that indeed internal generation of additional funds is usually possible, though time is needed to do to.

Externally generated funds

These fall, of course, into the two categories

1. *Debt.* This includes bank or other institutional loans, loans from other companies and debenture stock. This may be short ($\leq$ 1 year), medium (1 to 5 years) or long term (> 5 years) and loans may be *senior* (giving a primary claim on cash flow or assets for repayment) or *subordinated* (with secondary claim for repayment.

2. *Equity.* This includes ordinary shares, preferred shares and *hybrid* shares such as convertible (to preferred stock) bonds or shares with options (priority in buying new issues which may be exercised if, for example, the share price is to low).

A company is in a position to increase debt if:
a. Earnings are greater than interest payments.
b. It has strong and steady cash flow.
c. It has enough assets to cover (or secure) the debt.
d. Its debt levels are less than those of the OCS.

On the other hand equity might be more appropriate if:
a. The company needs to reduce debt.
b. Finance is required for long term projects.

Analysing financial decisions

In appraising funding options a useful basis is the following mnemonic:

F   Flexibility: options available, for example issue equity now and increase debt later.

R   Risk: how much debt can be afforded?

I   Income: can the interest payments be met?

C   Control: issuing equity dilutes the current ownership whilst debt is often secured against assets etc. which may be lost if debt payments are defaulted.

T   Timing: predictions for interest rates, share values etc. should be taken into account in funding plans.

Then in forming a financial plan these characteristics of proposed sources of funding should be compared to the company's BP (business policy), liquidity, OCS (optimal capital structure) and future cash needs.

Financing programs

These should include the following information:
1. A summary of the recommended program and its advantages.
2. A summary of why this program has been chosen.
3. A recommendation and rationale for an OCS.
4. Projection of amounts of funds required and when (based on a cash flow pro forma).
5. Sensitivity analysis of (4) - at least for the pessimistic case.
6. Detailed financing program giving the sequence of debt, equity or hybrid funding and the rationale for this.
7. A DCF (discounted cash flow) analysis of the plan giving the NPV of the company assuming the program is adopted.

1. BUSINESS FINANCE

Conclusion

Financing programs require careful comparison of the merits of internally and externally generated funds and of debt v. equity. Such programs should be in line with policy and the means of the company and be flexible.

BF6. Statistics and share values

Financial management decisions affect the value of a company's shares. Generally we hope to maximize the share value in the long term. In the short term, however, we would obviously prefer our actions to result in higher value.

In this context the *efficient market hypothesis (EMH)* is worth note. This takes three forms:

a. Weak form: current prices follow previous trends and historical factors.
b. Semi-strong form: current prices follow public information.
c. Strong form: current prices follow all information (that is including inside information etc.).

Of these it is usual to assume (b) and, indeed, somewhere between (a) and (b) would be a more realistic assumption for 'blue chip' stocks.

Risk and return

As an example, suppose that for company A the statistical data for one $10 share held for one year is:

Return, R_{ai}	$9	10	11	12	13
Probability, P_{ai}	0.1	0.2	0.4	0.2	0.1

Then the mean or expected return and the associated standard deviation are

(BF13) $(R_a)_{av} = \Sigma R_{ai} P_{ai} = \$11$

(BF'14) $\sigma_a = \sqrt{\Sigma (R_{ai} - (R_a)_{av})^2 P_{ai}}$

$= \sqrt{[(-2)^2 0.1 + (-1)^2 0.2 + (0)^2 0.4 + (1)^2 0.2 + (2)^2 0.1]}$
$= \sqrt{(1.20)} = \$1.095$ (10.95%)

Therefore zero profit is 1/1.095 = 0.913 standard deviations away from the mean. From a normal distribution table we see that the probability of this is 32%.

Hence the probability of zero profit is 18%.

For comparison consider a company B with $(R_b)_{av}$ = $11 and s_b = 7.12%.

Now zero profit is 1/0.712 = 1.404 from the mean and the probability of this is 42% so that p(0 profit) = 8%.

As an exercise the reader should confirm that p(> 20% profit) is 18% for A and 8% for B, illustrating that because it has greater σ or 'spread' A is more likely to make no profit but also more likely to make a profit.

Portfolio theory

In this the following assumptions are made:
1. Expected returns are normally distributed, an acceptable assumption for a portfolio but not necessarily for some members.
2. Investors are *risk factors* (as distinct from risk neutral or risk seeking).

Then the mean and standard deviation for the portfolio are given by

(BP15) $(R_p)_{av} = \sum x_i (R_{ii})$
(BF16) $\sigma = \sqrt{\sum\sum x_i x_j r_{ij} \sigma_i \sigma_j}$ (include i = j cases)

where X_i=MV of share i/($\sum$MV) ($\sum$MV=market value of portfolio)
r_{ij} = coefficient of correlation of returns on i, j ($r_{ij} = r_{ji}$, $r_{ii} = 1$)

For example, suppose the portfolio consists of two stocks and we have:

$X_1 = 60\%$, $(R_1)_{av} = 0.08$, $\sigma_1 = 0.04$
$X_2 = 40\%$, $(R_2)_{av} = 0.12$, $\sigma_2 = 0.06$

Then we obtain for the portfolio

$(R_p)_{av} = 0.6(0.08) + 0.4(0.12) = 0.096$
$\sigma_p = \sqrt{[(0.6)^2(0.04)^2 + (0.4)^2(0.06)^2 + 2r_{12}(0.6)(0.4)(0.04)(0.06)]}$
= 0.048   for r_{12} = 1 (perfect correlation + risk averaging)
= 0.04157 for r_{12} = 0.5 (risk is reduced)
= 0.03394 for r_{12} = 0   (risk is further reduced)
= 0 for r_{12} = -1 (perfectly negative correlation + zero risk)

calculating the standard deviation for various values of r_{12}, showing that the less the correlation between the two share values the less the risk (smaller σ) and the greater the advantage of a portfolio.

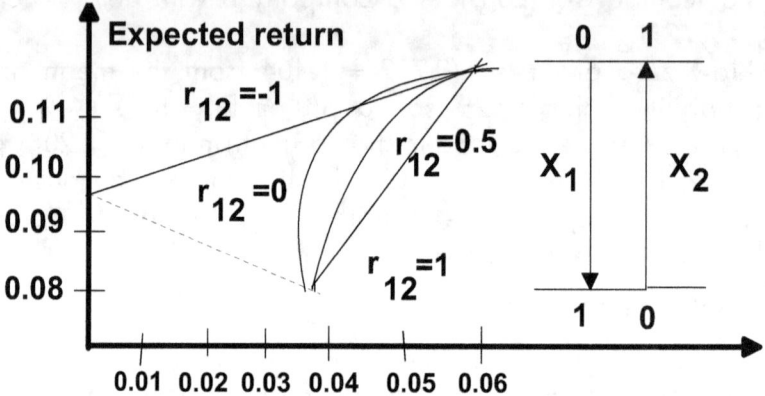

Fig. BF2 Effect of correlation coefficient

Figure BF2 shows the effects of varying the ratio of X_1 and X_2 and of various values of the correlation coefficient. It can be seen that for a given level of risk (σ) lower the correlation coefficient the higher the expected return. For the dashed line parts of the r_{12} curves an alternative point (at same risk) with a better rate of return exists, corresponding to a more profitable portfolio (with a higher proportion of X_2 which has a higher expected return).

Conclusion

Calculation of mean and S.D. (standard deviation) for a single share is a simple matter but may nevertheless be worthwhile. For portfolios the covariance terms are dominant in contributing to the S.D. of the portfolio. For a portfolio of 50 stocks, for example, these terms make up 90% of the S.D.

Thus when a new stock is added to a portfolio the covariance $C_{ip} = r_{ip} \, \sigma_i \, \sigma_p$ is of paramount importance and there is no risk reduction and hence point in adding a new stock for which $r_{ip} = 1$. Furthermore, for portfolios of more than 15 stocks the possible risk reduction in adding a new share is normally small.

BF7. Statistics and CAPM

In the capital asset pricing model (CAPM) the cost of equity is calculated as a function of the rate for risk free bonds (R_f) and the market rate (R_m), shown in Equation BF8.

For the purposes of the present discussion the market is a large portfolio and we assume
1. All investors can borrow/lend at the risk free rate R_f.
2. All investors have available to them the same estimates of R_{av}, σ and C for shares and the same *time horizon* for their investments.
3. A *perfect market* in which there are no constraints such as transaction costs.

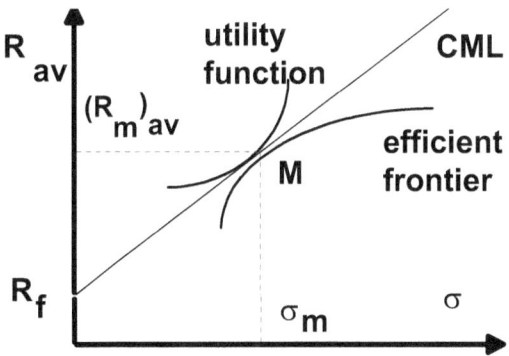

Fig. BF3 Market and investor curves

Figure BF3 shows the line corresponding to $r = 0$ in Figure BF2. This is the envelope of all points representing particular shares and is called the *efficient frontier* of the market as shares positioned on it have the best available return for given risk.

Figure BF3 also shows the *utility function* for a particular investor. This is a curve representing investor expected returns (hypothetical) for given risk. When this curve touches the efficient frontier the investor is prepared to buy at that point (and many others if the curves cross). The shape of the utility function shown is that for a risk averse investor.

Capital market line

This is the line drawn from R_f tangential to the efficient frontier (at point M which is the risk-return point for the market portfolio of risky stocks). The equation of the CML is

(BF17) $\qquad (R_p)_{av} = R_f + [\,(R_m)_{av} - R_f\,]\,(\sigma_p/\sigma_m)$

The CML shows the trade-off between return and risk for efficient portfolios. For individual stocks or inefficient portfolios the *security market line* is used and the equation of this (in the R-β plane) is

(BF18) $\qquad (R_i)_{av} = R_f + \beta_i\,[(R_m)_{av} - R_f\,] \qquad \beta_i = C_{im}/\sigma_m^2$

The beta value of the market portfolio is unity and stocks with a value less than one have lower risk whilst stocks with $\beta > 1$ have higher risk. As an example of this, Table BF4 shows values for some of Australia's largest companies.

Table BF4. Example Beta values.

Name	Beta	Industry
ACI International	0.651	Paper/packaging
ANZ Banking Group	0.854	Banking
BHP	0.958	Mining
Boral	1.088	Building materials
BTF Nylex	1.402	Industrial materials
CRA	1.458	Metals
CSR	1.004	Sugar refining
Coles-Myer	0.940	Retail
Comalco	1.339	Metals
Elders IXL	1.268	Real estate/food.
Goodman Fielder	0.848	Food
Lend Lease	1.243	Property developer
MIM	1.427	Metals
National Australia Bank	0.816	Banking
News Limited	1.606	Media
Pacific Dunlop	0.96	Tyres etc.
Pioneer Concrete	1.197	Building materials
TNT	1.535	Transport
Western Mining Corp.	1.502	Gold
Westpac Banking Corp.	0.896	Banking

The characteristic line

This is obtained by subtracting R_f from both sides of Equation BF18, giving

(BF19) $\quad \delta R_i = (R_i)_{av} - R_f = \beta_i \, [(R_m)_{av} - R_f \,] = \beta_i \, (\delta R_m)$

which is a straight line through the origin with δR_i = 'excess' return on asset *I* and δR_m = 'excess' return on market portfolio.

The characteristic line represents the *systematic risk* and this cannot be diversified away from because it depends upon factors which affect the whole market such as drought, war etc. Points not on this line, therefore, represent *unsystematic risk*.

Beta, therefore, is a measure of the systematic risk of an asset. Its values are more reliable if obtained from long term data and values for a large portfolio, rather than a single stock, are more stable, as might be expected.

Unsystematic risk

Actual data may, of course, be dispersed and linear regression is used to fit a characteristic line to observed data. The slope of this line is then the estimate of β_i.

The equation of the regression line can be written as

(BF20) $\quad (R_i)_{av} - R_f = \sigma_i + \beta_i \, [\,(R_m)_{av} - R_f \,] + e_i$

where e_i is an error term which corresponds to the scatter of the individual observations from the regression line.

The beta value for a portfolio of assets is given by

(BF21) $\quad \beta_p = \Sigma \, X_i \, \beta_i$

where X_i = MV of asset i/MV value of portfolio.

Then the S.D. of the possible returns of the portfolio is given, assuming no correlation of individual stock returns, by

(BF22) $\quad \sigma_p = \sqrt{[\, \beta_p^2 \, \sigma_m^2 + \Sigma \, X_i^2 \, \sigma^2(e_i) \,]}$

Then, as the number of stocks in the portfolio increases the size of the X_i^2 terms decreases and the contribution of the unsystematic risk (the second term on the right side of Equation BF22) decreases. This term tends to become negligible when there are 15 or more stocks, when the advantages of diversification have been achieved.

Empirical studies of CAPM

These have suggested that a slightly greater value than R_f should be used (in its place) but that additional non-linear terms are not needed in Equation BF8 (or BF18). Hence modified models in which R_f is replaced by $(R_z)_{av}$, for a portfolio of risky assets with $C_{zm} = 0$ are sometimes used. This variation is sometimes called the *two factor model*.

Another modification is to replace k_e in Equation BF6 with $k_e/(1 - f)$ where f is a factor based on the costs of share transactions.

Conclusion

The CAPM is a simple means of estimating the cost of equity where the beta factor is crucial as values of this vary considerably. CAPM is easily applied to portfolios and simple modifications which improve its accuracy are easily included.

BF8. Statistics and project evaluation

Here we include statistical considerations into the DCF (discounted cash flow) analysis of projects. Here the net cash inflows produced by a project for a given period are subject to *uncertainty* and there are a number of possible outcomes and to each of these we attach a probability. Doing this for three annual outcomes for a hypothetical case we obtain.

Table BF5.

	Year 1		Year 2		Year 3	
	p( )	income	p( )	income	p( )	income
	0.1	2,500	0.2	2,500	0.3	2,500
	0.25	5,000	0.25	5,000	0.35	5,000
	0.3	7,500	0.3	7,500	0.2	7,500
	0.35	10,000	0.25	10,000	0.15	10,000
$(R_t)_{av} = \Sigma R_p$	7,250		6,500		5,500	
$S_t = \sqrt{(R-R_{av})_p^2}$	2,487		2,670		2,570	

Then the mean and standard deviation for each period t are calculated:

(BF23) $\quad (R_t)_{av} = \Sigma R_t p_t(\ ), \quad \sigma_t = \sqrt{\Sigma(R_r - R_t)^2 p(t)}$

and the results are shown with the tabulation of the raw data for the annual outcomes.

Then the expected NPV of the project is given by

(BF24) $\quad NPV = -C + \Sigma(R_t)_{av}(1+k_f)^{-t} = -12000 + 7250/1.1 + 6500/1.1^2 + 5500/1.3^2 = 4095$

for which the standard deviation is given by

(BF25) $\quad \sigma = \sqrt{\sigma_t^2(1+k_f)^{-2t}} = \sqrt{2487(1.1)^{-2} + 2760^2(1.1)^{-4} + 2750(1.1)^{-6}} = 3700$

if the cash flows in each period are independent of those in others. In practice this is unlikely as most projects have overall budget constraints.

Then the S.D. when the cash flows are perfectly correlated (giving the greatest degree of dispersion) is given by

(BF26) $\quad \sigma = \Sigma \sigma_t(1+k_f)^{-t} = 2487(1.1)^{-1} + 2670(1.1)^{-2} + 2570(1.1)^{-3} = 6398$

and the S.D. where the cash flows are less than perfectly correlated lies between the two values given by Equations BF25 and BF26.

Alternative approaches

Alternative methods of approaching this type of problem include:

[1] *Simulation.* In this approach values of each variable (for example the income in year 1) are selected randomly and the known pdf for this variable 'consulted' to determine the probability of the value. Carrying out such *perturbations* many times (say 100) an approximate pdf for the NPV of the project can be determined.

1. BUSINESS FINANCE

[2] *Sensitivity analysis.* In this selected variables are perturbed to give an idea of the sensitivity of the model to these variables. This in turn may suggest which variables should be more carefully constrained in planning and controlling a project.

Investment decisions

Knowledge of the risk or uncertainty of a project is particularly useful in decision making. For example, suppose that we have for two projects A and B the following data:

Project	NPV	σ	σ/NPV
A	5,000	2,000	0.4
B	1,000	1,000	0.5

On the basis of this simple information we should choose project A as the preferred project as it gives a higher return with lower relative risk.

The CAPM and project evaluation

We have seen that uncertainty in stocks can be represented by plots with *risk-return* coordinates, that is, R v. σ, as shown in Figs BF2 and BF3. Equivalently, and more convenient in practice, we can use coordinates R and β (see Equation BF18). Then when market equilibrium exists all risky securities plot on the *security market line (SML)*.

Then, as an example, assume a company A is contemplating a project Z and the risk return coordinates for this and the company are as shown in Figure BF4.

When A undertakes project Z the risk-return point of the company will lie on line ZA, the exact point depending upon the scale of the project relative to the size of the company.

As this is above the SML, giving higher return for given risk than the market, investors will bid up the shares in A until 'A+Z' plots on the SML.

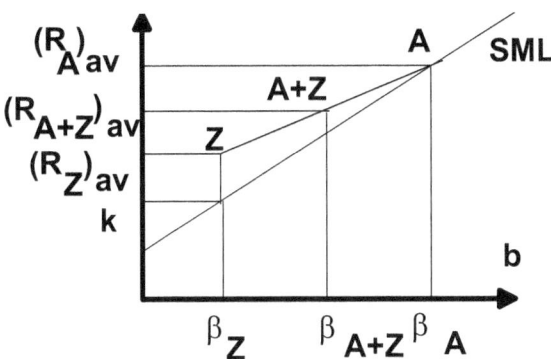

Fig. BF4. R-beta plot for co. A and project Z

This implies that projects should be accepted if they plot above the SML, the equation for which is

$$(R_i)_{av} = R_f + \beta [(R_m)_{av} - R_f]$$

from which it follows that the discount rate, k_z for the project Z is

(BF27) $\quad k_z = R_f + \beta_z [(R_m)_{av} - R_f]$

This is the rate necessary to compensate investors for a risk β_z and it is because $(R_z)_{av} > k_z$ that the project is acceptable.

This provides a useful means of evaluating risky projects.

For example if project Z has $\beta = 1.25$, the risk-free rate is 8% and the market premium is 4% then the required rate of return for the project is

$$k_z = 8 + 1.25(4) = 13\%$$

and the NPV of the project is calculated using this rate.

Conclusion

The CAPM provides an important modification for DCF analysis, the discount rate k_z which gives more realistic NPVs than, for example, k_f.

Note that when there are variations in k_f these can be included in the k_z and in turn NPV calculations and that combinations of risky projects are usually assumed risk independent and their NPVs calculated separately.

BF9. Current asset management

We have discussed investment in shares or long term projects. A priority financial consideration, however, is current asset management and this too involves investment or funding. As a crude analogy here, it is important to keep the ship going as well as to decide upon its destination!

Current assets and the operating cycle

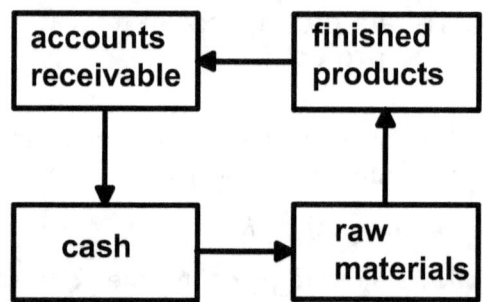

Fig. BF5 Credit based operating cycle

The operating cycle by which assets are 'turned over' is illustrated in Figure BF5 for the case of a company which offers credit terms on its sale.

This is for the case of a manufacturer who 'transforms goods in kind' and, of course, the objective is to minimize delays in the cycle and to maximize the quantities involved in it (subject to certain limits or constraints).

When credit is not issued the accounts receivable in a 'triangular cycle' and for the case of a retailer the finished products and raw material activities are merged into 'goods', resulting in a 'line cycle'.

The importance of current assets is illustrated by the proportion of current assets to total assets shown for Australian companies in Table BF6.

1. BUSINESS FINANCE

Table BF6. Current assets as a percentage of total assets for industry groups during 1973-74 to 1976-77.

Current assets	Manuf-acturing	Wholesale	Retail	Services	All industries
Inventory	23.1	29.2	27.9	22.8	23.8
Cash	0.94	0.76	1.34	2.41	1.2
a/c's receivable	16.2	24.3	14.2	15.4	16.3
Total	40.4	54.7	44.9	40.4	41.3

Clearly current assets are a very significant part of a company's assets. In managing current assets we seek to:
1. Determine optimum levels of assets to be held. Adding a 'safety margin' to this we obtain the amount of current assets to be held.
2. Finance this asset holding, first distinguishing between the minimum or permanent current asset holding required (which should be as little as possible) and temporary asset holdings required to deal with such factors as seasonal variations in trade.

These and other considerations, such as company policy in relation to current assets and, for example, credit sales, form the agenda for management of current assets and the financing of them.

Inventory management

Inventory management involves stocking raw material, work in progress (some proportion of which can be classed as inventory for accounting purposes) and holdings of finished goods.

Quantities of inventory required depend upon demand levels, the production process ('high tech' processes for example, may have different requirements to those of basic 'hands on' processes) and its duration, and also upon the price and durability of the goods (for example holdings of perishable goods, must, of course, be minimized rigorously).

The costs of inventory management include the following:
1. Acquisition costs, that is costs of 'set-up' of warehouses etc., the costs of the ordering process (staff time etc.), shipping and handling costs and, in some cases, foregone costs when quantity discounts offered by a supplier are not utilized (this is called an *opportunity cost*).
2. Carrying costs. These include the foregone interest income associated with the cost of inventory held, rent paid for storage space (and also rent forgone for space owned by the company which could have been rented out), interest charges, costs of deterioration and obsolescence and, in the case where prices are falling, the surplus price paid.
3. Stockout costs. These are the cost of lost sales and loss of customer goodwill (if not loss of long term customers) and production hold ups.

Hence the costs of inventory are often somewhat hidden costs more associated with non-productive use of funds which we should seek to minimize.

Economic order quantity

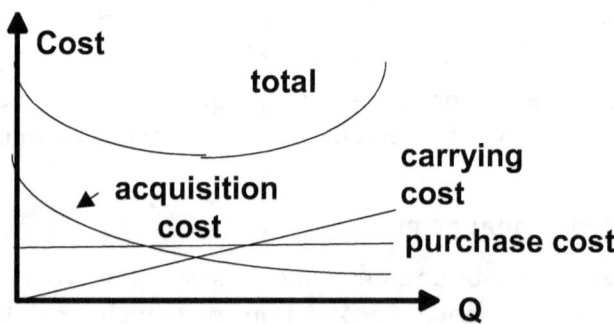

Fig. BF6. Economic order quantity.

As carrying costs of inventory are directly proportional to the quantity held whereas the acquisition costs decrease when inventory is ordered in larger lots, the total of these two costs has a minimum called the *economic order quantity*, as shown in Figure BF6.

1. Business Finance

The economic order quantity is easily determined by defining Y as the demand per unit time for the product and P as the unit price of the product. Then the total cost of inventory purchase is $= YP$ per period.

Then if X is the order size (the number of units ordered at a time) the number of orders per period (month, year etc.) $= Y/X$.

If the cost per order is A, then the total acquisition cost per period is $= AY/X$.

Finally, if carrying cost per unit is C, then the total carrying cost $= (X/2)C$, that is the cost for the average number of units stocked.

Then summing these purchase, acquisition and carrying costs per period we obtain

(BF28) $\quad T = YP + (Y/X)A + (X/2)C$

Taking the first derivative, that is dT/dX, and putting this equal to zero we obtain

$X = \sqrt{(2YA/C)} = EOQ$

In turn we can now calculate Y/X, the associated order frequency.

Equation BF28 can also be applied to production processes when, if A = cost of setting up for production, the value $\sqrt{(2YA/C)}$ is the *optimum production run* size (and Y is now the 'production demand' and C the unit production cost).

Note, however, that in practice the EOQ has a range, as does, of course, the demand Y. In addition, when quantity discounts apply, the EOQ should be calculated for both the normal and discount prices.

Liquid asset management

Liquid assets are moneys held in currency or bank accounts, that is, *cash,* and short term securities and other assets that can be converted to cash immediately. Liquid assets must be held for day to day operations, for example for transactions such as payments of accounts owing. Some proportion of liquid assets held should be as a precaution against unexpected cost increases etc. and sometimes it is advantageous to use such liquid assets for speculation on the stock market as a means of increasing company revenue.

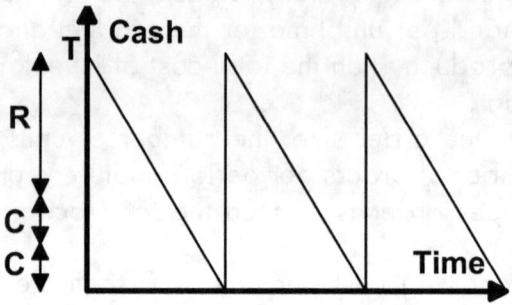

Fig. BF7 Cycling of liquid assets

Liquid assets involve costs such as those of issuing shares, overdraft charges and forgone interest (accounted for as the WACC k_0). Thus liquid assets behave in the same way as inventory, periodically requiring 'top up', as shown in Figure BF7.

Here initial liquid asset holdings are R dollars in cash and one or more 'bundles' of short term securities worth C dollars. Then, when the $\$R$ has been spent a bundle of securities is sold to replenish the cash supply.

Then the bundles of securities correspond to order size in Equation BF28 so that C is given by

(BF29) $\quad C = \sqrt{(2Tb/i)}$

where i is the short term interest rate and b is the transfer cost of converting $\$C$ of short term securities into cash, and R is given by

(BF30) $\quad R = C + T(k_w + k_d)/i$

where k_w = cost (cents) of withdrawing $\$1$ of invested funds and k_d = cost of investing $\$1$ in short term securities.

Note that this result does not allow for cash stockout, which should in any case be avoided, or uncertainty in cash requirements, though of course it would be counterproductive to attach uncertainty to more variables than necessary in financial management.

It is also argued that the simple model here is unrealistic in many countries where companies usually use a bank overdraft rather than hold liquid assets to finance part of their operations. Some middle course, at least, on this point is probably preferable.

Accounts receivable management

Accounts receivable is money owed to the company from sale of goods or services on credit. Here it is necessary to distinguish between *trade credit,* which is often on more favourable terms than *consumer credit,* often involving quantity discounts and no interest charges or service fees, whereas consumer credit may involve cash discounts or interest charges and service fees in providing credit.

Costs of accounts receivable management include accounting costs, forgone interest on cash held in accounts receivable, cost of bad debts which must be written off (the accounts), cost of delinquent (late) debts (forgone interest etc.) and establishment costs for customer accounts.

It is important to have a clear *credit policy* which must include such matters as acceptance criteria (for giving credit), credit limits and terms and collection policy (instalments v. lump sum etc. and measures taken on late payments).

Commonly credit is given by a *factoring company* which charges from two to four % interest on the total accounts held in the name of the company issuing credit and factoring companies usually required a minimum credit parcel of $M0.5. Usually a *non- notification agreement* is entered into whereby accounts are sent out under the selling company's name. The factoring company then holds the debtors' ledger and takes the risk for bad debts.

An alternative means of financing credit is by *accounts receivable financing* whereby finance is via a loan, usually form a finance company which is pledged the receivables as security. Finance companies will usually lend up to 70% of any bad debts (if the full amount were repaid there would be little incentive to collect the debt).

Credit cards are a means by which a limited factoring service is offered to retailers at a service charge ranging from 1.5 to 5%. The use of these is a satisfactory proposition for a retailer if the resulting increase in sales is greater than the cost of credit and if it is cheaper to use credit cards than to provide one's own credit.

Commonly used financial ratios

In the field of financial management many financial ratios are used as a measure of company liquidity, profitability etc. These include:

1. *Current ratio* = total current assets/total current liabilities. This is used as an indication of ability to pay short term debts.
2. *Quick ratio* = (cash+securities+a/c's receivable)/(total current liabilities - overdraft). This is a better indicator of immediate needs than (1)
3. *Inventory turnover* = annual sales/average inventory.
4. *Average collection period* = average receivables/average daily credit sales.
5. *Total asset turnover* = sales/total tangible assets.
6. *Debt to total assets* = total liabilities/total assets.
7. *Earnings coverage ratio* = EBIT/interest costs. Here EBIT is 'earnings before interest and taxes'.
8. *Profit margin on sale* = net profit after taxes/sales($).
9. *Return on shareholders' funds* = net profit after taxes/shareholder's funds.
10. *PE ratio* = price/earnings (per share) ratio for shares.

Conclusion

Current asset management is a very important part of company management and determination of such quantities as the 'EOQ' is vital as significant savings may result in the long term. In addition the means by which assets are held and credit given, for example, are important considerations and the alternatives should be carefully considered.

1. BUSINESS FINANCE

BF10. Sources of finance

There is a market for finance called the *capital market* and the principal finance providers in this are:

1. *The Reserve Bank.* This has limited powers but can affect the capital market considerably by its actions. Its funds are the *statutory reserve deposits* it holds from the trading banks.

2. *Trading banks.* The dominance of these in the market is not what it once was and these now hold only about 20% of the total assets of financing institutions in Australia. The reserve Bank can control the trading banks to some extent by the amount of the statutory reserve deposits (SRDs) it requires of them and by requiring them to maintain a specified *LGS ratio* or proportion of liquid assets to total deposits (usually about 18%).

3. *Authorized short term money market dealers.* These are mostly insurance companies or overseas companies. There are as many of these as trading banks.

4. *Merchant banks.* There are mostly subsidiaries or offshoots of broking houses, life assurance companies, subsidiaries of trading banks or overseas companies. There are about 100 such companies.

5. *Finance companies.* These have the same origins as (4) and there are about 100 such companies at present. Some, for example, are allied with particular motor car manufacturers.

6. *Life assurance companies.* These are made up of insurance companies, investment funds, superannuation funds and overseas companies. The latter require government approval to commence operation in Australia. There are about 50 'life' companies.

Each different type of 'player' in the capital market has a particular role and good financial management demands a familiarity with the different services and options for finance which they provide.

1. BUSINESS FINANCE

Short term finance

Companies require short term finance principally to fund current assets when these require boosting for a limited period. Short term finance is often called *bridging finance* as it is frequently used to allow a project to commence or continue while long term finance arrangements are being negotiated. Then, as soon as the long-term finance becomes available, the bridging loan is redeemed.

The principal means of short term finance are:

1. *Trade credit.* This accounts for roughly 15% of a typical company's liabilities + equity and nearly 50% of its short term finance. Whilst trade credit is not negotiated etc. it is a de facto form of finance. Wholesale companies, for example, use more trade credit (about 40% of their ST finance) than do manufacturing companies (about 30%) because they need to hold more current assets.

2. *Trading banks.* These provide ST finance in:

(a) *Overdrafts.* Banks issue an overdraft facility with an account with a limit and a rate penalty (calculated daily) and usually require some asset security and that a company have a satisfactory current ratio.

Overdrafts are often used to buy assets at bargain prices or loans on call and banks prefer that overdrafts are *fully fluctuating* (between 0 and L/2 where L is the limit).

When funding requirements are medium term banks may lend via a *fully drawn account*, rather than an overdraft, and these require slightly higher rates and regular repayments for a fixed period of, say, five years.

Another alternative arrangement is a *bill acceptance facility* whereby the bank agrees to act as an acceptor of bills issued by the company up to a specified amount.

(b) *Short term mortgages.* These are given at a higher rate than the overdraft rate and are usually to finance property or industrial development.

(c) *Lease finance.* This is at a significantly higher rate than overdraft rates but the use of lease finance has grown considerably in the last decade or so.

3. *Merchant banks, finance companies and authorized dealers.* These are sources of short term loans or mortgages. They also act as factoring agents, deal in the commercial bills market (that is sale of bills held under a bill acceptance facility between financial institutions), and are particularly active in lease financing and installment credit (to companies which sell goods on installment terms to cover their current asset needs).
4. *Intercompany loans.* Some companies with seasonal cash surpluses, for example, lend to companies with temporary cash needs. Later in their business cycle such companies may also need to borrow on the intercompany market and such arrangements are often semi-permanent.

Long term finance: equity

Companies usually fund themselves initially through issuing of shares. This provides long term finance which may be supplemented when the need arises by debt finance. Initial equity finance is obtained by *floating* a new or existing proprietary company. This is done by applying for stock exchange listing and this is granted subject to conditions such as minimum numbers of shares and shareholders required. It is further required that the public hold a substantial proportion of the issue.

Floats are sometimes private, that is funded by institutional investors, but it is usually necessary to 'go public' to attract sufficient investors to qualify for listing. Floats, therefore, are nearly always a public issue of ordinary shares, and this is one of several ways in which equity finance can be obtained. These include:

[1] *Initial issue of ordinary shares.* Usually with the advice of financial institutions the total value of the company is decided upon. Then the share price is set, from which the number of shares to be issued follows.

In setting the share price the price/earnings ratios of similar companies should be considered. If, for example, the company is expected to earn 10 cents per share and the PE ratio of similar companies is between 10 and 15, a share price of between $1.00 and $1.50 is indicated.

The cost of a public float is substantial, including advisory services, preparation of prospectus, legal fees for the latter, accounting fees, printing etc. and stock exchange charges. In addition, however, the issue should be underwritten, usually by the advisory financial institution, typically a merchant bank or broking house. Here, for a fee usually from 1 to 4% of the issue price the issue is guaranteed and the underwriter will take up any unsold shares, sometimes by enlisting sub-underwriters, these then being sold to their institutional clients.

[2] *Subsequent issues of ordinary shares.* When a company requires additional equity finance it can make a further issue of ordinary shares. Such issues may take several forms, including:
a. *Rights issues.* Here each shareholder is entitled to an additional number of shares proportional to his current holding. Usually the issue price is below the current market price to ensure that shareholders are keen to take up the rights. They are then able to resell the rights to obtain a short term gain. If the issue price is close to the market price, however, it is usual to have the issue underwritten.

As an example, suppose a company makes a one in four rights issue, that is $N = 4$ shares entitles to one additional share, and that the issue is at a subscription price $S = \$1.50$ whilst the market share price $= M = \$2.00$. Then the value of one right is given by

(BF31) $\quad R = N(M - S)/(N + 1) = \$0.40$

Then if a shareholder has 1000 shares he can sell his rights for 1000 x 0.4/4 = $100 or exercise his right and take up 250 shares at a cost of $375. If he takes the first option it would seem that he has made money for nothing, but in practice the share price is likely to fall. If it falls to $1.90, for example, the loss in the value of his holding is exactly balanced by the value of his rights. Thus there is still motivation to exercise his right to increase his share holding at a 'bargain' price.

b. *Private issues.* A private issue of ordinary shares is a 'placement' of shares with institutional investors such as life companies, pension funds and investment companies. Such issues can be accomplished quickly, cheaply and at a price close to (but still less than) the market price. As the market price will be affected, however, private issues should be made only with the approval of shareholders except where expediency and urgency demand funding.

c. *Bonus issues.* When a company has spare funds, for example as a result of asset revaluation, it may make a bonus share issue. If this is, say, a 'one for one' issue we should expect the market value of the shares to halve. Such a share split does not alter the paid-up capital of a company and requires only a book entry in the balance sheet. Usually, however, the share value is not reduced in proportion to the 'dilution' of the shares resulting from the bonus issue and hence the company's market value is increased. Thus, whilst the issue has not raised equity, it has raised the value of the existing equity.

d. *Share options.* These are an option to buy a specified number of shares at a stated price by a given date. Then, if the share price of the company increases, option holders stand to gain by exercising their options.

Options are sometimes issued to employees as an incentive to greater participation and productivity and sometimes they are attached to an equity or private debt issue as a 'sweetener', in the latter instance in return for better interest rate terms, for example.

e. *Internal equity finance.* The equity sources of long term finance discussed thus far are all external. Internal equity finance is also important. This is moneys resulting from profits (after tax and dividends, if any), to which may be added depreciation charges (in some cases upward revaluation makes these a positive contribution), the final result being *retained earnings.*

Such retained earnings provide a 'free' source of long term finance when reinvested but there is an associated opportunity cost (interest rates etc. which could have been charged by investing the funds elsewhere).

1. BUSINESS FINANCE

Long term finance: debt

Debt finance is less costly than equity finance because interest is paid before dividends are considered and loans are usually secured against assets. Hence lenders are subject to less risk than shareholders and thus will accept a lower rate of return. The cost advantage of debt is increased by its tax deductibility. The disadvantage of debt funding is the greater risk and, if repayments are defaulted, creditors may seek liquidation.

Debt finance can be obtained in various ways, including:

[1] *Short to medium term loans (up to ten years)*.

a. *Bank term loans.* Trading banks provide term loans for periods of up to 10 years for capital expenditure needs of rural, industrial, commercial and export development. The rates are usually slightly higher than the overdraft rate and fixed for an initial period and variable thereafter. Security in the form of charges over assets or the guarantee of an overseas bank or parent company is usually required.

b. *Term loans from government agencies.* Such agencies of government as the Australian Resources Development Bank (ARDB), created to assist major mining and other development projects, the Australian Industry Development Corporation (AIDC), which assists industrial development, and the Commonwealth Development Bank, which was initially intended to assist smaller primary producers and manufacturers, provide alternative sources of term loans for special purposes.

c. *Eurodollar loans.* A Eurodollar loan is negotiated in US dollars and channeled to Australia through the European banking system. Other currencies may be dealt with in the same way or via their country of origin. Increasing numbers of companies use overseas finance which is sometimes cheaper, though an interest rate penalty is involved and exchange rate fluctuations can affect the repayments required.

d. *Other financial institutions.* Term loans may also be obtained from merchant banks (or a consortium of these), finance companies (at a fairly high rate) and life companies (from which more favourable terms may be obtained if the company holds the company superannuation fund, for example).

[2] *Long term debt finance* (more than ten years)

a. *Mortgage loans.* The major sources of mortgage loans are life assurance companies, pension funds and trustee companies. Typically companies use such loans to finance their own buildings and plant. Rates and terms of such loans vary considerably and, for example, initial repayments of principal may be delayed for a number of years until the project develops a cash flow.

b. *Debenture and unsecured notes.* Debentures are issued in units (usually $100) and sold in bundles and are secured against specified assets. Unsecured notes are issued in the same way but without security but usually at a higher rate of interest than debentures (in turn marginally less than mortgage funds).

Debentures are secured either by a *fixed* or *floating charge* over assets. The latter is usually preferred by companies as stamp duties involved in specifying the assets over which a fixed charge is made are avoided. In addition they are free to dispose of assets and replace them with other, perhaps more attractive ones.

Debenture issues are usually made for one of three maturity dates, what is short term (2 - 4 years), medium term (5 - 8 years) and long term (10 -15 years).

When debentures are issued a *trust deed* states the terms of interest and principal repayment, the security for the loan (usually a floating charge), restrictions required of the borrowing company such as limits on its further borrowing or sale of assets, and the limits of liability of the company. A trustee is then appointed to hold the deed and oversee company operations to ensure that the terms of the deed are met.

c. *Negative pledge lending.* To avoid the restrictions of trust deeds unsecured loans are often obtained with a negative pledge provision which prohibits future loans on a secured basis without offering the holder of the negative pledge the same security. The terms of such loans often involve restrictions on dividend payments and financial ratios such as the current asset ratio. As these are in the company interest, however, they are less inhibiting than the asset restrictions of trust deeds.

Hybrids of debt and equity

[1] *Preference shares*

Preference shares receive priority in payment of dividends and in capital payments in the event of liquidation. Three conditions that may be attached to preference shares are:

a. *Redeemable* or *non-redeemable*. Redeemable shares are equivalent to debentures and may be automatically redeemable or at the company's option. Irredeemable preference shares are similar to ordinary shares.

b. *Cumulative* or *non-cumulative*. If the shares are cumulative the company is obliged to pay preference dividends not paid in previous years before paying ordinary shareholders. Such arrears payments are not required if they are non-cumulative.

c. *Participating* or *non-participating*. Participating shares entitle their holders to a dividend greater than the preference dividend rate in a very profitable year. Non-participating shares do not participate in profit sharing other than by the prescribed dividend rates.

In practice preference shares are usually irredeemable, cumulative and non-participating. Preference shares are usually issued at a higher dividend rate than the debenture interest rate because debentures have priority of payment. This high cost has discouraged the use of preference shares in Australia in the past.

[2] *Convertible notes.*

These are unsecured notes that can be converted into shares at maturity, carrying a fixed interest rate in the interim, and if the holder does not convert he must be repaid at face value. Conversion is at a price specified in the notes and, assuming that the ultimate market price of the company's shares will be higher than this convertible notes do involve a value which may be attached to the option to convert.

Conclusion

There are many sources and types of equity and debt finance and study of the various options is worthwhile. The balance of a company's equity and debt financing, along with many other factors such as policy, it also important and the question of optimal capital structure is discussed further in the next section.

1. BUSINESS FINANCE

BF11. Capital structure decisions

The market value of a company (V) is the sum of the total market value of its equity (E) and debt (D), that is:

(BF32) $\quad V = E + D = NOI(1 - t_c)/k_0$

where NOI is the company's net operating income and k_0 and t_c are defined with Eqn BF6 which was

(BF33) $\quad k_0 = k_e(E/V) + k_d(1 - t_c)(D/V)$

Then the *optimal capital structure* is that value of D/E which minimizes k_0 (the weighted average cost of capital or WACC) and maximizes V.

As an example consider a company with NOI = $10,000 which is 'unlevered' (that is $D = 0$). This income is to be distributed to shareholders who hold 100,000 shares of 50 cents (hence the earnings per share are 10 cents) at a rate $k_e = 13\%$. Then the value of the company is calculated in column (a) of Table BF7, assuming $t_c = 0$.

In this case, because $D = 0$, the required rate of return on equity capital (k_e) is equal to k_0, that is

$$k_0 = NOI / V = 10{,}000/76{,}923 = 0.13$$

Now assume that, rather than issuing shares only, 60,000 shares at 50 cents and $20,000 worth of 8% debentures are issued. Assuming the market value of the debt remains at the issue price and the shares increase in value to $1 (from 77 cents in case (a)), then if the rate of return required by shareholders is 14% the value of the company is as calculated in column (b) of Table BF7.

The WACC of the company is now given by

$$k_0 = 0.14(60/80) + 0.08(20/80) = 0.125$$

showing a slight decrease from case (a).

1. Business Finance

Table BF7. Examples of different equity/debt mixes.

	(a)	(b)	(c)
NOI	10,000	10,000	10,000
k_d (Σ debts)	0	1,600	2,000
Σ dividends	10,000	8,400	8,000
k_e	0.13	0.14	0.2
E	76,923	60,000	40,000
D	0	20,000	25,000
V	76,923	80,000	65,000

Finally, if the company issues 50,000 shares at 50 cents and $25,000 worth of debt at 8% and the shareholders require a rate of return of 20% then the market value of the company is as calculated in column (c) of Table BF7. Here, as a result of the increase in debt funding, it is assumed that the share price has dropped to 80 cents (from $1 in case (b)).

Now the WACC of the company is given by

$$k_0 = 0.20(40/65) + 0.08(25/65) = 0.154$$

and the market value of the company has decreased whilst the cost of capital has increased as a result of a further increase in debt, as illustrated in Figure BF8.

Here the cost of capital is reduced by the cheaper debt finance diluting the equity finance. The cost of equity increases, however, resulting in an optimum capital structure (OCS).

Modified models

Modified models which seek to better reflect the behaviour shown in Fig. BF8 have been proposed, for example in which it is proposed that k_0 in Equation BF33 should be a constant which is a measure of a company's risk and that the cost of equity should be calculated as

(BF34) $\qquad k_e = k_e^* + (k_e^* - k_d)(1 - t_c)(D/E)$

where k_e^* is the required return on equity when the company is financed only by equity (that is, $D = 0$).

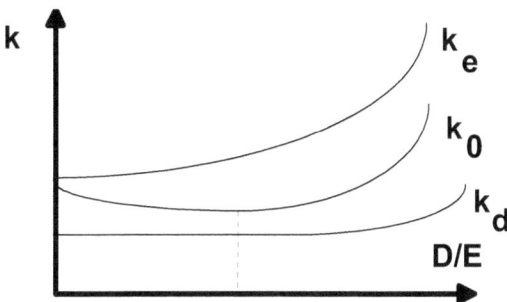

Fig. BF8 Optimum capital structure

Neither such modified models nor the original CAPM model take into account the tax advantages of using debt or the risk factors associated with increased debt, however, but the original model of Equation BF33 is, for conceptual purposes at least, still preferred.

Conclusion

The CAPM model of Equation BF33 is, conceptually at least, still very useful and Table BF7 provides a good example of how a minimum value of the WACC and an associated maximum value of the company might occur at some optimum value of *D/E* corresponding to the optimal capital structure.

Indeed companies and sometimes share markets act as though an OCS exists though the assumption that the cost of equity rises as D/E rises is not entirely logical.

Nevertheless the search for the OCS is a worthwhile one and it should be based on earnings before interest and taxes, earnings per share, ability to service debt and like factors with a view to maximizing the market value of the company and the return on investment of investors.

1. BUSINESS FINANCE

BF12. Share price and curve plotting

In this final section an example of a simple but widely used technique for plotting day by day share prices to determine appropriate 'buy and sell' points is discussed. Then examples of how data for simple curves may be tested by linear plots are given. These are intended as exercises at this point but may initiate some thinking about whether share prices and the like can have determinable turning points or asymptotes.

Plotting share prices

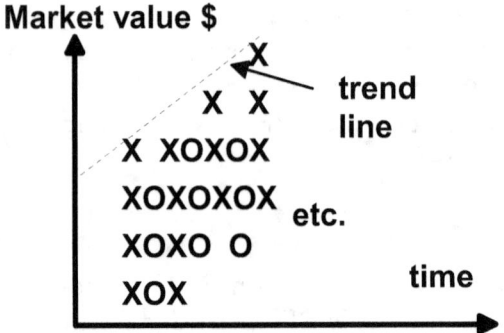

Fig. BF9 Three point reversal method

A simple example of a commonly used method of plotting share values is the *three point reversal* method, originally employed with the New York market (appropriate adjustment to 'x', rather than three, points is therefore needed in application to other share markets).

This involves plotting a *point and figure* chart as shown in Figure BF9. In this a new column is used when there is a reversal in price and dates can be marked on the time axis for, say, each month.

Then in the three point reversal method a reversal is when there is a price change equal to three squares on the chart, the chart being plotted as one square = $1 for prices above $20, one square = 50 cents for prices less than $20 and so on.

Then, with a little experience it is possible to identify patterns which indicate good points at which to buy or sell shares. There are many such patterns, however, and such techniques require a great deal of experience.

Such study of reversals and their pattern is usually applied to industrial shares. For commodities, on the other hand, trend lines like that shown in Figure BF9 are generally used to indicate likely outcomes. These, however, only signal 'up' and not 'how far?' and such techniques as those discussed in the remainder of the chapter are potentially useful.

Curve plotting techniques

The method of linear regression (by least squares) is widely used to obtain a 'line of best fit' to observed data. Many spreadsheet packages (e.g. Excell, Quattro, and 123) do this for you and the reader should try them on the data $(x,y) = (1,20)$, $(2,30)$, $(3,40)$ when they should find the coefficient of correlation (c.c.) to be 1, the 'intercept' = 10 etc., i.e. we have a straight line. In the interim, however, two useful examples of how this may be achieved graphically are given.

[1] **Rectangular hyperbola**

The equation of this hyperbola is $y = ax/(b + x)$ which can easily be rearranged to give

$x/y = (b + x)/a$

so that if we plot (x/y) against x the straight line of Figure BF10(b) is obtained and the magnitude of the intercept with the x axis = b whilst, or more interest, the inverse slope of the line equals the asymptote of the hyperbola.

This, the *Mohr plot*, is useful in estimating an asymptote or 'ceiling' value towards which it may be suspected that some variable is converging.

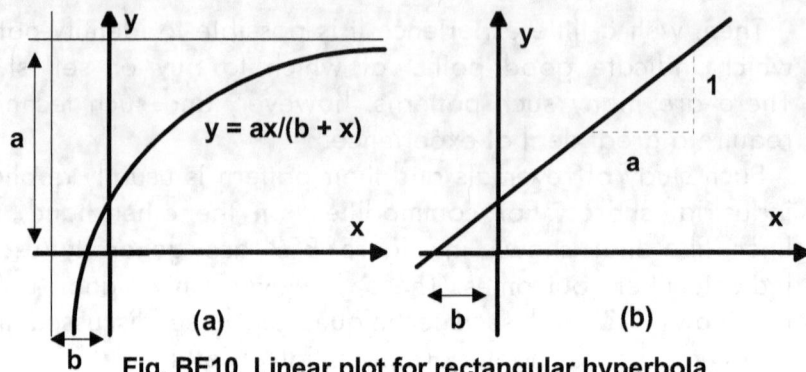

Fig. BF10 Linear plot for rectangular hyperbola.

[2] Parabola

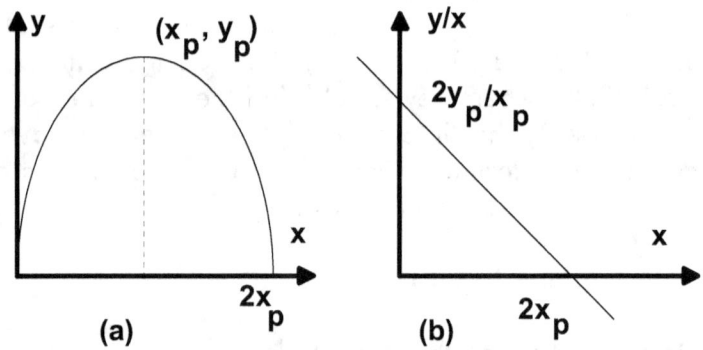

Fig. BF11. Linear plot for a parabola

Figure BF11(a) shows a parabola passing through the origin, turning at (x_p, y_p) and passing through the x axis again at $2x_p$. The equation for this parabola can be written as

$$y/x = (y_p/x_p)(2 - x/x_p)$$

so that if we plot (y/x) against x the straight line shown in Figure BF11(b) is obtained.

Then the intercept of this line with the x axis = $2x_p$, the intercept with the y axis = $2y_p/x_p$ whilst the slope of the line is equal to $-y_p/x_p^2$. Therefore this type of plot is useful in estimating a turning point in a variable when one is suspected.

[3] Other possible curves

Many other possible curves might be considered but in econometrics, for example, where attempts are made to fit functions to economic variables it is found that for most purposes functions of parabolic form are sufficient.

The reason for this might be understood if we examine an infinite polynomial, taking the exponential function as an example:

$$e^x \text{ or } \exp(x) = 1 + x + x^2/2! + x^3/3! + x^4/4! + \cdots$$

Then, within a range, square terms (or a parabola) are all that is needed to approximate a curve and practical functions in such fields as economics are not likely to rise much more steeply than $y = x^2$ or to oscillate like sin( ) or cos( ). Oscillations do, of course, occur, but not with sinusoidal regularity and we are more likely to study individual oscillations using plots such as that of Figure BF11(b). Note too, in passing, that with suitable rearrangement of terms a linear plot can also be established for $y = \sqrt{x}$.

Conclusion

In a chapter on business finance where a good deal of discussion has been about share prices and uncertainty in these some mention, however brief, of the many techniques for plotting share price variations is appropriate though it is not possible to give recommendations on how such charts might be 'read'.

In this context graphical plots which reveal asymptotes and turning points are hopefully worthwhile.

Exercises

[1] Given the data: $(x,y) = (1,7), (2,12), (3,15)$ plot y against x and guess the peak or turning value of y_p. Repeat using another scale. Compare the two guesses. Then plot y/x against x and use the results in Figure BF11 to find the turning point. (Ans: x = 4, y = 16).

[2] An application of exponential growth laws which has a similar spirit to the compound interest formula (which has been described as the very basis of capitalism) is *Mohr's Law of Money,* namely that if the rate of making money is given by
d$/dt = (constant =)$a$
where a = *activity*, and if a = (constant = k)$,
the we obtain the exponential growth law:
$ = (constant) e^{kt}
and it is interesting to consider what values of the constant are comparable to substantial rates of interest in the compound interest formula.

References

Aitken M, Brown P, Izan H, Kua A, Walter T. An intraday analysis of the profitability of trading on the ASX at the asking price. *Australian J. Management,* vol. 20, no. 2, 1995.

Aitken P. *10 Minute Guide to 1-2-3 97 for Windows.* QUE, Indianopolis, IN, 1997.

Anthony RN, Govindarajan V. *Management Control Systems,* 8th ed. Irwin, Chicago, 1995.

Backer M, Jacobsen LE. *Cost Accounting.* McGraw-Hill Kogusaka, Tokyo, 1964.

Bruce R, McKern B, Pollard I, Skully M. *Handbook of Australian Corporate Finance,* 3rd edn. Butterworth, Sydney, 1989.

Bongiorno C. *The Australian Dividend Handbook.* ANZ/McCaughan Research, Melbourne, 1993.

Cunningham C, Nikolai LA, Bazley JD. *Accounting: Information for Business Decisions.* Dryden Press, Orlando FA, 2000.

Cohen AW. *Three Point Reversal Method of Point and Figure Stock Market Trading,* 8th edn. Chartcraft Inc., Larchmont NY, 1982.

Day JX. *Your Money and Your Life.* Lothian. Melbourne, 1989.

_____. *Shares,* Jan. 1999. Fairfax publications, Melbourne, 1999.

Fiske WP, Beckett JA. *Industrial Accountant's Handbook*. Prentice-Hall, Englewood Cliffs NJ, 1954.

Garrety MD. *Making Money in The Futures Market in Australia*. M.D. Garretty, Toorak, Melbourne, 1979.

Green I, Murray B. *Test Questions in Accounting with Suggested Solutions,* 8th edn. VCTA Publishing, Melbourne, 1990.

Hewat, T. *The Intelligent Investors Guide to Share Buying*. Wrightbooks, Melboure, 1988.

Lang T, McFarland WB, Schiff M. *Cost Accounting*. Ronald, New York, 1953.

Lewis M. *Liar's Poker: Two Cities, True Greed*. Hodder & Stoughton, London, 1989.

Magnus A, Scorgie ME. *Financial Management, Concepts and Calculations*. LaTrobe University, Melbourne, 1998.

Microsoft Excel Users Guide, V 3.0. Microsoft, Redmond VA, 1991.

Microsoft Excel Function Reference, V 3.0. Microsoft, Redmond VA, 1991.

Microsoft Excel Database Access User's Guide, V 4.0. Microsoft, Redmond VA, 1992.

Mohr G.A., *Elementary Thinking for the 21st Century,* Xlibris, Sydney, 2014.

Mohr GA, *The Scientific MBA,* 5th edn, Balboa Press, Bloomingon, Indiana, 2017.

Mohr GA, *Elementary Thinking for Modern Management,* Amazon-Kindle, 2018.

Naish PJ. *Summit Book of Investment*. Evans Bros, London. 1968.

Newbold P, Bos T, *Introductory Business Forecasting*. South-Western, Cincinnati OH, 1990.

O'Leary TJ, Williams BK, O'Leary LI. *McGraw-Hill Microcomputing Labs.* McGraw-Hill, New York. 1992.

Peirson G, Bird R, Brown R. *Business Finance*, 4th edn. McGraw-Hill, Sydney, 1985.

_____. Proc. Australian Society of Accountants 1980 State Congress. Aust. Soc. Accountants, Melbourne, 1980.

_____. *RSA Computer Literacy and Information Technology.* Heinemann, Oxford, 1988.

Seiler RA. *Principles of Accounting: A Managerial Approach.* Charles E. Merrill, Columbus OH. 1967.

Wilkinson-Riddle GJ. *Accounting Level III.* McDonald Evans. Plymouth. 1982.

Williams LR. *How I Made One Million Dollars Last Year Trading Commodities.* Windsor Books, Brightwaters NY. 1979.

Wu FH. *Accounting Information Systems.* McGraw-Hill, New York. 1984.

Chapter 2

INTERNATIONAL ECONOMICS (IE)

> *In economics, hope and faith coexist with great scientific pretension and also a deep desire for respectability.*
> JK Galbraith, *New York Times Magazine*, 7 June 1970.

In this chapter *macroeconomics* is discussed. This is usually concerned with the national economy of a country but necessarily includes consideration of *international economics* (the 'big E' as it is sometimes called). In contrast, *microeconomic* deals with economics at corporate level, that is with *managerial economics*, and this is discussed in the next chapter.

IE1. Introduction

In this section a few introductory economic principles and concepts which are generally pertinent in any discussion of economics are introduced.

Economic progress

Economics these days is generally discussed in much the same fashion as the weather and with similar pessimism. It is worth noting that since 1900 production per capita has increased fourfold and the length of the working week has been reduced by 30% in industrialized countries.

Economic problems

Current economic problems include unemployment, inflation, the poor, the environment and 'undesirable production', that is, production of goods and services which are socially and economically destructive.

2. INTERNATIONAL ECONOMICS

The role of government

There are various schools of through on just how great a role government should play in economics. Adam Smith (1776), the pioneer of modern economics, favoured a totally free market with no tariffs etc. Keynes (1936), on the other hand advocated government creation of jobs and a greater government role in the economy. This was a relatively moderate position, however, compared to that of Marx who advocated ownership by the workers (not by the state as is commonly supposed).

Today, however, some mix of these three points of view exists. There must be some element of social policy for the disadvantaged whilst debate over the relative merits of *Keynesian economics* versus those of the *monetarists* (who hold that the government should only 'fine tune' the controls of a free market economy) continues.

Economic goals

What are our economic goals? These are likely to include dealing with high unemployment, achieving price stability, production efficiency, equitable distribution of income and economic growth. Additional qualitative factors which should also be considered are the environment and individual economic freedom and security.

Specialization

It is because individuals specialize their work that we need *exchange* and hence money. This introduces economies of scale into our activities. Here a simple example of *comparative advantage* is relevant.

Suppose a doctor who earns $50 per hour takes one hour to mow the lawn. To have a gardener do it, on the other hand, costs $5 per hour but the gardener takes two hours to do the job. Which is the best option?

At first sight some would say that the doctor should mow the lawn himself and save $10. This involves an *opportunity cost*, however, of $50 which the doctor could have made by staying in his office another hour and has forgone. The example is somewhat trivial but does demonstrate *comparative advantage*.

2. INTERNATIONAL ECONOMICS

Resource constraints

As an example of the application of *resource constraints* suppose we wish to maximize the total production P of a product by two processes, x and y, and that these processes cost \$4 and \$5 per unit respectively. Then if this is subject to the constraints (i) that the total cost be not more than \$32 and (ii) that not more than 6 units can be produced using process x, we state the problem mathematically as

(IE1)   Maximize $P = x + y$
            subject to $4x + 5y \leq 32$ (i)
                          $x \leq 6$ (ii)

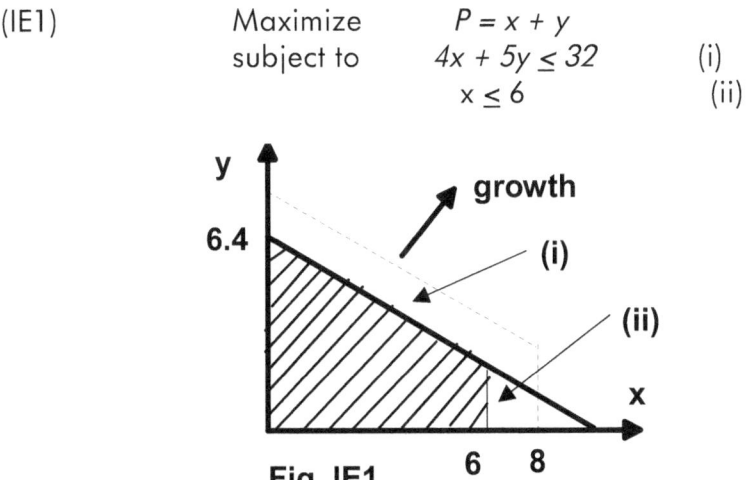

Fig. IE1

This is, in fact, a *linear programming* (LP) problem and the solution is obtained graphically in Figure IE1. Here the shaded area is the *feasible region* and this is bounded by the axes and the two constraints.

The solution will be one of the corner points of the *simplex* formed by the constraints and it is easily found that the maximum occurs at $x = 6$, $y = 1.6$ (giving the maximum $P = 7.6$).

Generally, the boundary given by (i) and (ii) is called the *production possibilities curve* (PPC) which grows as shown in Figure IE1 if allowed.

2. International Economics

Economic planning

In economic planning it is, of course, important to consider both short and long term goals and frequently some balance must be struck between these. For example, a fundamental question is whether it is better to encourage spending on capital goods (for example building factories etc.) or permit spending on consumption goods (output from existing factories).

The former (capital goods expenditure) will provide long term growth in the economy at the price of short term deprivation. Generally, therefore, some balance between the two extremes must be struck.

Conclusion

Economics is the study of how people, company's and countries make a living and of the problems associated with so doing. Much progress has been made and much remains to be made and definition of economic goals should be made with sensible constraints in mind, as well as due consideration of both short term and long term effects.

Finally, whilst the mathematical details of economics are important tools, some of the fundamental questions such as the degree to which government should be involved remain matters of debate.

IE2. Supply and Demand

The law of *supply and demand* is well known and is usually stated along the lines "supply rises to meet demand" and this, as far as it goes, is true. This does not, however, tell us why this happens. In the following section supply and demand curves are discussed along with the effects on these of imposed controls, government and business policies and other considerations.

2. INTERNATIONAL ECONOMICS

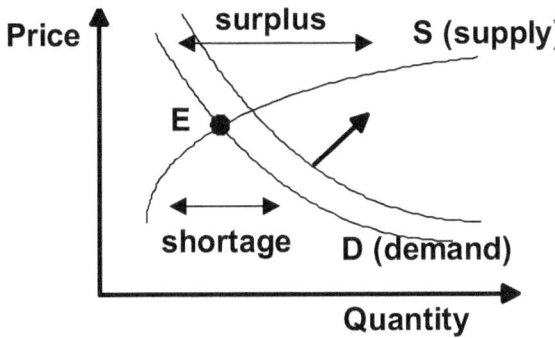

Fig. IE2 S & D curves

Figure IE2 shows typical supply and demand curves for which it is frequently assumed that there is *perfect competition*, that is there are many buyers and sellers and none are able to influence the price individually. Then the result is called a *competitive market*.

Here the supply goes up as the price goes up because the supplier is more motivated to produce more goods. The S curve, therefore, is drawn from the point of view of the *supplier*.

The demand curve, on the other hand, goes down as the price goes down because with a greater quantity of goods available competition forces the price down (or conversely shortages result in increased prices). Hence the D curve is drawn from the point of view of the buyer.

Then the point of intersection of the two curves, E, is called the *equilibrium point*. Below this point demand exceeds supply and there is a shortage and above it supply exceeds demand and there is a surplus, as shown in Figure IE2.

If there is an increase in demand, as shown in Figure IE2, then there is an increase in the equilibrium price P_E. Clearly, therefore, S & D curves show a good deal of information.

2. INTERNATIONAL ECONOMICS

Introduction of controls

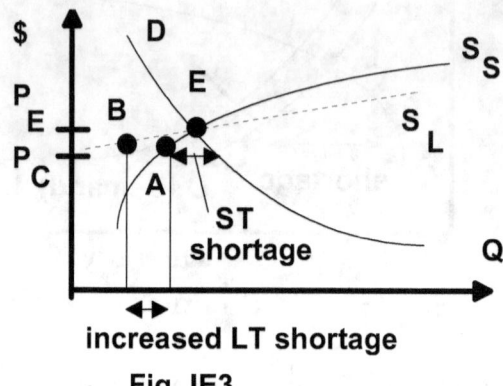

Fig. IE3

What happens if arbitrary price controls are introduced? This provides a useful example of the application of S & D curves. Suppose, for example, a ceiling price P_C is placed on the product. Then, as shown in Figure IE3, we move down the (short term) supply curve S_S to a point A and there is a short term shortage.

Further, in the long term suppliers will reduce supply for given price giving a new and 'flatter' supply curve S_L. Operation then moves to a point B in Figure IE3, so that the shortage increases in the long term.

Elasticity of supply and demand

The *elasticity* of supply or demand is given by the slope of the corresponding curve, that is by

(IE2) $\qquad e = (\delta Q/Q)/(\delta P/P)$

and is comparable to the definition of many similar quantities in science.

A particular example is the aggregate labour market which is often assumed to have a vertical supply line, there being a fixed number of available workers (or zero elasticity). When the size of the work force increases, therefore, so that this labour supply line moves to the right, it quickly follows that wages *(P)* will fall.

2. INTERNATIONAL ECONOMICS

Optimum production

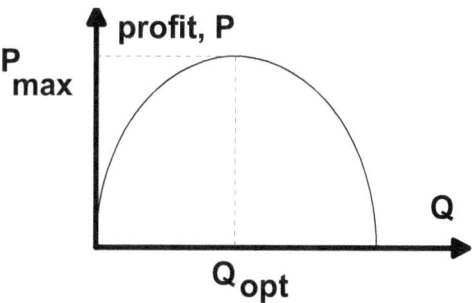

Fig. IE4. Optimal production

In the present context it should be noted that there are limits to which production can be increased as well as optimal production rates which must be considered.

Figure IE4 shows the profit (per item) v. quantity produced (Q) curve for a production process. Here P increases at first as set up costs etc. are 'spread' until constraints come into play and P decreases. Then a maximum marginal profit occurs when the production quantity = Q_{opt}.

As the marginal profit P = marginal revenue (MR) - marginal cost (MC) clearly P_{max} is obtained when MC = MR.

Then in a very competitive market (in which the elasticity e is high), it can be seen from the well known result

(IE3) $P - MR = P/e$

that P = MR = MC.

Hence we can conclude that in a very competitive industry production is close to MC (exceeding it slightly by P/e).

Effect of government

Government affects supply and demand in various ways, including:
1. It purchases goods and services.
2. Through *transfer payments* (welfare etc.) which are largely spent, thereby increasing demand.

3. Through taxes, including federal, property, sales, personal and company taxes. Such *receipts* take money out of the system.
4. Through *expenditure* on education, welfare, roads etc.
5. Through regulations and controls which affect interest and tax rates etc.

Effects of business

The business sector affects supply and demand in the economy in such ways as the following:
1. By purchasing goods and services, thus creating demand.
2. By production, creating supply.
3. Through imports and exports.
4. Through the stock market, levels of activity influencing economic growth, currency exchange rates etc.
5. Through the capital market, levels of activity influencing exchange rates, interest rates and economic stability.

Conclusion

Supply and demand curves have useful application as we have already seen and many more applications will be seen later. Consideration of factors such as labour supply and efficient production rates is, in this context, of vital importance, as is an understanding of the various ways in which government and the business sector can influence supply and demand.

IE3. National product and national income

National product is the dollar value of goods and services in a year and national income is the sum of all income derived from providing these goods and services, including wages and salaries, rents, interest and company profits. These are discussed in detail and applications of these measures are discussed in the following section.

Gross national product (GNP)

GNP is one of the most widely publicized economic yardsticks and is defined as the sum of several terms, namely:

(IE4) $$GNP = C + G + I_g + X - M$$

where $C = NP$ = personal *consumption* and expenditures
G = government purchases of goods and services (not including transfer payments such as social security benefits)
I_g = gross domestic investment (plant and equipment, including inventories)
X = exports of goods and services
M = imports of goods and services

Because of the need to allow for depreciation a net national product is defined as

(IE5) $NNP = GNP - \text{depreciation} = GNP - (I_g - I_n)$

where I_n = net private domestic investment = I_g - depreciation.

Then national income (NI) is given by

(IE6)   NI = NNP - sales taxes
≈ PI = NI - (co. + soc. sec. taxes) + transfer payments
and   DI = PI - personal taxes

where PI = personal income and DI = disposable income (spent on interest payments or consumption or saved).

Finally, defining the *consumer price index* (cpi) as the weighted average price increase through the whole economy (%), the *'real GNP'* is given by

(IE7)   real GNP = (nominal GNP)/(1 + cpi/100)

Example

As an example consider the effect on GNP of the Keynes proposition that increased government expenditure should be used to reduce unemployment.

2. INTERNATIONAL ECONOMICS

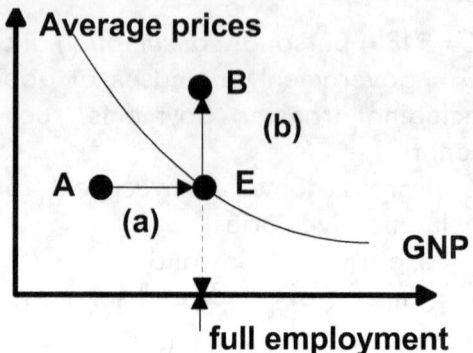

Fig. IE5. A Keynesian argument

This is illustrated in Figure IE5. Here increased government spending has resulted in an increase in demand which shifts us from point A to an equilibrium point E (hence we have shifted to another demand curve).

There may then, however, be a further increase in demand as a result of increased competition (by those now employed etc.). This will result in an increase in price and we move to point B in Figure IE5. Hence inflation has resulted and moves to curb this will reduce employment, the by now all too familiar cycle.

To give a measure of step (a) in Figure IE5 Keynes defined a *consumption function* C, from which follows the *marginal propensity to consume (MPC)* and *marginal propensity to save (MPS)*:

(IE8) $\qquad MPC = \delta C/\delta DI, \quad MPS = \delta S/\delta DI$

and *MPC* is the slope of the consumption function whilst *MPC* + *MPS* = 1.

Then, supposing we have *MPS* = 0.2, and increase in government spending (δG) of \$M100 will result in $\delta GNP = \delta G/MPS = $ \$M500 (using the second of Equations IE8).

This *multiplier effect* of savings is very important, though hard to believe from the simple equations given here. The point is, however, that if *MPS* = 1 there is no such effect and it is consumption which brings about the effect in question.

2. International Economics

Fiscal policy

The foregoing discussion of GNP considers only variation of G and its effect. To generalize how government *fiscal policy* affects the GNP we write the budget *(B)* in terms of revenue *(R)* and expenditure *(G)* as

(IE9) $B = R - G$

and if $R > G$ (surplus), for example as a result of higher taxes, then demand is reduced and the cpi drops.

If $R < G$ (deficit), on the other hand, the deficit spending may stimulate the economy in the short term at the expense of greater government debt.

If this increase of $G = \delta G = \$M100$ and the tax rate is $t = 25\%$ (i.e., 0.25) we amend the multiplier effect calculated above to

(IE10) $\delta GNP = \delta G/[MPS(1 - t) + t] = \$M333$

so that inclusion of tax (or an increase therein) reduces the effect on the economy (this phenomenon is called *fiscal drag*).

Then in formulating fiscal policy the aim should be to 'juggle' R and G in such a way as to achieve full employment and then balance the budget (so that $R = G$) when that objective has been attained.

Conclusion

GNP is a simple quantity but less simple are the supply and demand considerations involved in fiscal policy which involve questions of employment levels, government spending, tax rates and inflation, to name a few.

On the question of government spending it is probably worth noting as an aside that costs of security (defence, police etc.), education, welfare (social security and health) and infrastructure are, of course, very high indeed, not to speak of administration costs both internal and external to these. In economies where government is largely responsible for these activities, therefore, it should be able to control events to a considerable extend by fiscal policy.

2. INTERNATIONAL ECONOMICS

IE4. The Financial System

The financial system of banks, stock exchanges etc. is the machinery by which the economy runs. Important parts of this machinery include the following:

The Money Stock

The money stock in the economy is the total currency *in circulation* (that is, in public hands) plus the total of *demand deposits* (that is cheque accounts etc.). This total is denoted M_1 and a second total $M_2 = M_1$ + the total of savings/business accounts = M_1 + 'near money' is also defined as a measure of the money stock.

Liquid assets

A liquid asset is one which can be converted into money (M_1) readily at little cost at its 'proper' value.

The Reserve Bank

The reserve bank might be termed the 'banks' bank' as it holds the *statutory reserve deposits (SRDs)* of the trading banks, a set ratio called the *reserve ratio (R)* of their total deposits. Its excess reserves are its total reserves less the SRDs.

Suppose, for example, $R = 0.2$ and \$M10 is deposited by a customer in a bank. The bank now has excess reserves and can create \$M10/0.2 = \$M50 worth of additional demand deposits.

This occurs because the bank can lend \$M8 to a customer who passes this (by cheque) as payment for property etc. to a customer of another bank who deposits the cheque. This second bank can now lend 80% of this amount and so on, so that we obtain a series of demand deposits resulting:

(IE11) δD = original deposit + 80& of latter + 80% of latter - - -

$$= 1/[1 - (1 - R)] = 1 + (1 - R) + (1 - R)^2 + \text{- - - -}$$

This then is the crux of how the banking system works and the reason why the multiplier effect discussed in Section IE3 does actually occur.

2. INTERNATIONAL ECONOMICS

Interest rates

The reserve bank can affect interest rates by buying government bonds, decreasing their supply and thence forcing up their price. This in turn reduces their interest rate and banks may follow suit and cut their *prime rate* (the rate on their safest loans).

The discount rate

This is the rate the reserve bank charges the trading banks when it makes loans to them. By increasing this or the reserve ratio to tighten the money supply the reserve bank might seek to slow down an 'overheated' economy, for example.

The stock market

The reserve bank can influence the stock market by, for example, increasing the discount rate, in turn leading to a general increase in rates which in turn may lead to a fall in the stock market.

Common examples of such policy are:

(a) Expansive monetary policy.
Here the reserve bank buys bonds causing reduction in interest rates and in the MPS (marginal propensity for saving). Thus greater demand is stimulated causing an increase in the GNP (which includes the multiplier effect of Equation IE10).

(b) Restrictive monetary policy.
Here the reserve bank sells bonds causing an increase in rates and in the MPS. Thus demand is reduced, causing a decrease in the GNP (again including the multiplier effect).

Note here that increase in price of securities is assumed to cause a reduction in their interest rate. This is because for a $100 bond with a yield of 8% the present value if it has a ten year term is given by

$$PV = 8/r + 8/r^2 + 8/r^3 + \text{- - - - } + (100 + 8)/r^{10}$$

where $r = 1 + i$ and i is the market interest rate. From this it is clear that if the market rate increases then PV decreases and vice versa.

Conclusion

The multiplier effect related to Equations IE8 is of importance not only in the overall economic system as Equation IE10 shows, but also in the banking system, as shown by Equation IE11. In turn, this part of the sequence of events, which the reserve bank can trigger off by intervention in the securities market etc. Such monetary policy, the 'monetarists' (as distinct from the 'Keynesians') argue, should be the limit of government powers in what should otherwise be a free market economy.

IE5. Aggregate demand

We have now seen two ways of controlling the economy, one being fiscal policy, that is a positive δG acting as an 'injection' to stimulate the economy, as illustrated by Equation IE10. This is the Keynesian approach. In the opposition camp are the monetarists such as Friedman who argue that only monetary policy is necessary to fine tune what should otherwise be a free market economy. Here we shall briefly discuss both approaches.

Monetary policy

The aim of monetary policy is to control the economy by controlling the money supply, in turn affecting interest rates, which in turn affects investment *(I)* and hence aggregate demand *(C + I)*.

Figure IE6 shows the marginal efficiency of investment or investment demand curve, that is the amount businesses will invest at various interest rates.

Then, as described in Section IE4, expansive monetary policy, as it causes a reduction in interest rates, leads to an increase in investment demand and hence in aggregate demand and we move down the 'MEI' (marginal efficiency of investment) curve.

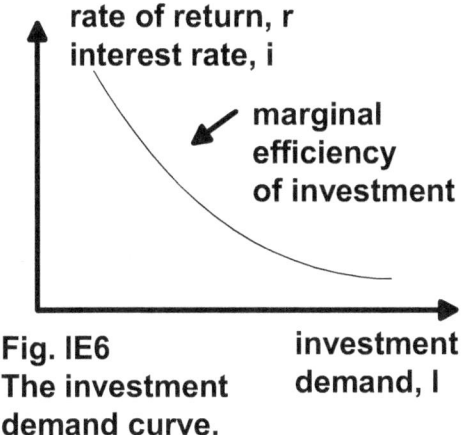

Fig. IE6
The investment demand curve.

The classical economic theory of the *velocity of money (V)* is in line with this approach. This theory is based on an *equation of exchange:*

(IE12) $MV = PQ$

where
  M = the quantity of money in public hands
  P = average level of prices
  Q = quantity of output
  V = velocity of money = number of times M is spent to buy Q during the year

and V is defined as equal to PQ/M and taken to be approximately constant (so that Equation IE12 is a tautology).

Then monetarists argue that the authorities should increase the value of M by a fixed percentage each year (and figures from 2 to 4% are suggested). This will give a corresponding growth in Q and hence GNP.

2. INTERNATIONAL ECONOMICS

Fiscal policy

Fiscal policy was discussed in Section IE3 where it was shown that an increase in government spending δG leads to a 'multiplier effect' increase in GNP.

Those who have doubts about this approach, however, argue that deficit budgeting (via an increase in G or reduced taxes) and borrowing to finance that deficit will decrease I (domestic investment) and hence aggregate demand. In the case of an increase in G (as advocated by Keynesians) this result is called *crowding out*, that is government investment displaces private investors from the market.

Monetary policy v. fiscal policy

The best policy would seem to be to use a combination of both approaches and to thus have a 'two pronged' approach.

For example, we might choose to have:

a. Fiscal expansion (an increase in G)
b. A low growth in M (giving some restraint)

using 'unused' growth in M and borrowing part of the finance for δG from the private sector, thereby aiming for lesser increases in I (and hence growth in GNP) and a more stable system.

Exercise

As an exercise discuss the following propositions concerning reducing unemployment:
1. Income splitting between spouses before tax when there is only one bread winner.
2. Keeping tariff barriers for certain areas of activity.
3. Reduce the average working week to 35 hours &/or 4 days
4. Export incentives (tax breaks or other).
5. Lower interest rates to promote business.
6. Making first home mortgages part tax deductible to stimulate business in the building industry.
7. Reduce the retirement age:
(a) Across the board
(b) In certain industries (hazardous etc.), circumstances (injury etc.).

2. INTERNATIONAL ECONOMICS

8. Add any others that come to mind.

As an example of (1) consider:
a. husband income = $60k, tax = $20k
wife income = $30k, tax = $10k
total net income = $60k
b. husband income = $60k, tax = $10k ($10k spouse allowance)
total net income = $50k (+ expenses of spouse working saved)

This doesn't sound too bad from the point of view of the family but the government now collects only a third as much tax from this couple but will collect tax from another worker replacing the wife in the workforce and, in addition will save social security payments for that worker. There is also a social benefit to the family and the person taken off the dole.

Conclusion

A study of aggregate demand has provided a means of comparing the classical monetarist and Keynesian (fiscal) points of view on economic policy.

It would seem clear that some middle course might be the best one, making the best use of whatever controls that we have.

In speaking of growth in GNP etc., it is perhaps worth remembering that oft quoted growth rates of 2% and the like (by politicians etc.) are really only treading water in the face of population increase, if that, and with unemployment an enduring problem in what were once the strongest economies there is a need for a reappraisal of such matters as taxation and deficit budgeting to support greater demands by 'green', educational, business or other groups. In addition such measures as a shorter working week, less tax for single bread winners (supporting spouses) and tax and other incentives for industries that are likely to create sought after employment might help.

2. INTERNATIONAL ECONOMICS

IE6. Aggregate Supply

The backward 'L' result AEB in Figure IE5 can be taken as a supply function because as employment/output increase so does price. If the steps of this Keynesian *aggregate supply* function are plotted on axes rate of inflation (%) and unemployment (%), respectively vertical and horizontal, we obtain a special L shaped case of the *Phillips curve*. In other words, we reverse the GNP axis in Figure IE5 and relabel it unemployment, also reversing AE by moving A to the right of E.

The Phillips curve was based on nearly 100 years of statistical data (up to 1957) for the UK and takes the form shown in Figure IE7(a).

Calculations based on this data suggested that with unemployment at about 2.5% wage inflation would remain in the range 2.5% to 3%, just offsetting growth in GNP so that price inflation would be zero.

For a decade (until 1966) the Phillips curve held well but thereafter began to come adrift and in 1968 Friedman developed the concept

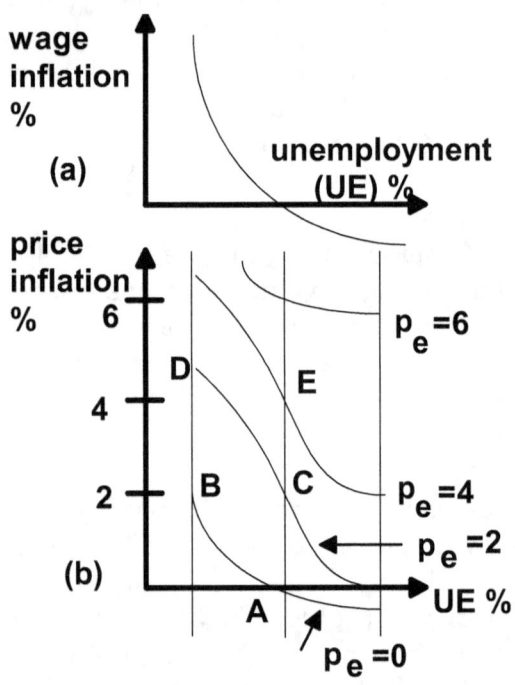

Fig. IE7. Phillips curves

of the *expectations augmented Phillips curve* shown in Figure IE7(b). Here we begin at point A, the 'natural' rate of unemployment (of which estimates range from 4% to 10%). Now if the government increases money supply, causing greater aggregate demand which in turn increased prices, then unemployment is reduced and we move to point B.

74

2. International Economics

Now inflation is around 2% and p_e = expected inflation = 2% causing pressure for increase in 'real wages' and we move to point C, the increase in wages causing increased unemployment.

Then if another injection of funds into the money supply occurs the process is repeated and we move from point C to point D, and thence to point E, and so on.

Hence a *cost-push* (prices and wages) or *demand-pull* (high demand) cyclic behaviour results called an *inflationary spiral*.

As this phenomenon did occur for many years in some countries the augmented Phillips curve does work well in showing how continued monetary policy of a 'catch up' kind can cause even more trouble.

Conclusion

Solutions to the sorts of problems illustrated by Figure IE7 might include wage indexation (to the cpi), freer markets (elimination of monopolies etc.), price surveillance, tariff reductions and the like. But we have heard this BS before and some would have it that we must be prepared to accept that a 'natural' rate of unemployment of near 10% may be appropriate in modern economies and that it is cheaper to pay people the dole than create government jobs of a relatively unproductive nature in offices which would be more costly to provide than dole payments.

This is to forget the problems of the 'boom and bust' nature of the system whereby *recessions* (decline in GNP for two consecutive quarters in seasonally adjusted terms) and *depressions* (greater than 10% unemployment for two consecutive years) are accepted too easily. The latter question is discussed in Section IE7 and the question of unemployment is returned to in Section IE12.

2. INTERNATIONAL ECONOMICS

IE7. Economic Instability

Economic instability, witnessed by bearish and bullish markets, slumps, recessions, depressions and booms is an all too familiar fact of life. In the following section we briefly outline the nature of the business cycle and examples of factors which contribute to it. Discussion of alternative approaches to smoothing out economic cycling is then given in the following section.

The four phases of the business cycle

Table IE1. Illustration of the *acceleration principle*.

Period	Phase	(1) Sales thousands	(2) Lines = (1)/10,000	(3) $\delta(2)$ = net investment	(4) (3) + 2 = gross inv.
1	steady	200	20	0	2
2	steady	200	20	0	2
3	expansion	220	22	2	4
4	expansion	240	24	2	4
5	peak	250	25	1	3
6	peak	250	25	0	2
7	recession	230	23	-2	0
8	recession	210	21	-2	0
9	trough	200	20	-1	1
10	trough	200	20	0	2

As an example consider a manufacturer whose sales are shown in column (1) of Table IE1. Suppose that a new assembly line is required to produce 10,000 units of produce. Then the required number of lines is shown in column (2). The net investment required is then the *change* in column (2) and this is shown in column (3). Finally, supposing that equipment replacement requirements are that two lines are replaced each period. Then the *gross investment* required is then column (3) + 2 and this result is shown in column (4).

2. INTERNATIONAL ECONOMICS

Then, as Table IE1 shows, a smallish increase in sales (typically 3 to 10%) doubles gross investment, a phenomenon called the *acceleration principle*. It is such phenomena that give rise to instability in the economic system.

In the case of investment, therefore, some 'lag' in funding tends to smooth out such problems. In other words when an increase in sales occurs it is desirable to assume that it will only partly be sustained in basing investment decisions on that increase.

Factors contributing to fluctuations

Factors which affect the business cycle and its stability include:
1. Changes in consumer spending or saving.
2. Changes in net exports ($X - M$).
3. Changes in government spending (remember the multiplier effect).
4. Fiscal and monetary policy.
5. Interest rate changes (and in turn inflation rates).
6. Political factors, such as 'election budgets'.

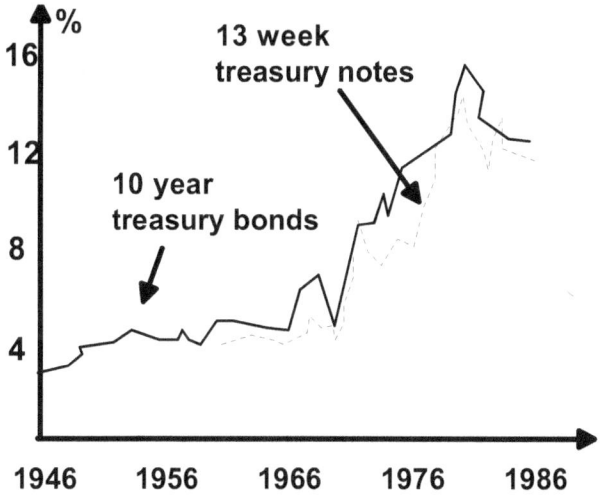

Fig. IE8. Australian government bond yields

2. INTERNATIONAL ECONOMICS

As an example, Figure IE8 shows the yield rate of Australian government bonds for the period 1946 - 86. Whilst over the long term there is a general upward trend the shorter term fluctuations are on occasions very sharp.

Particular events during that period were the OPEC initiated oil crises of 1973 and 1979 in which a large and sudden increase in oil price forced importers of oil to borrow heavily from banks, it turn causing inflation, in turn raising the oil price. Arguably the effects of these can be seen in Figure IE8.

Beneficiaries of fluctuations

At the national level boom and bust behaviour of the economy and its market benefits certain people, for example:

a. Currency exchange dealers knowingly benefit from instability.
b. Import/export companies may unwittingly benefit.

Both parties may also contribute to instability, as may politicians etc. via wars and other disruptions.

At the international level major economies such as those of the USA, UK, Germany and Japan have a major influence, as do organizations such as the IMF and EEC, of course.

Whether 'globalization' of economics will result in a more stable system is a moot point, however, and it seems unlikely that individual countries can ever be guaranteed stability.

Conclusion

Economic instability is much discussed and in much the same vein as the weather. Nevertheless the question of satisfactory control mechanisms is an important one and this is taken up again in the following section.

Having mentioned the 1973 and 1979 oil shocks, however, one cannot help but wonder what further events of a similar, if not related, kind are in store in the future. By then, hopefully, a better insulated system will be in place.

2. INTERNATIONAL ECONOMICS

IE8. Fine tuning or stable policy settings?

Whether we choose to use fiscal (Keynesian approach) of monetary policy or a combination of the two to regulate the economic system it is still important to decide whether this should be done using periodical 'fine tuning' adjustments or by putting in place fairly rigid policy rules

The fiscal or Keynesian approach is to increase aggregate demand $(C + I)$ and thereby stimulate the economy via the multiplier effect of Equation IE10 with a view to creating full employment.

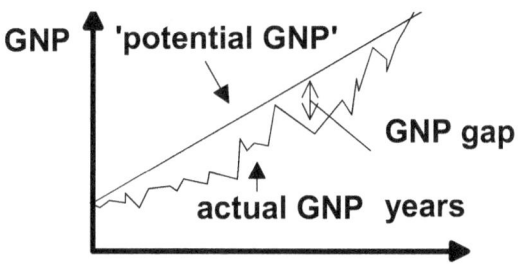

Fig. IE9. The GNP gap.

Then periodic fine tuning is used to eliminate the GNP gap shown in Figure IE9, this being the shortfall from a target GNP (set, for example, with the aim of full employment). Setting such targets, however, requires the use of forecasts which in turn require appropriate data and techniques for evaluating it.

Forecasting

Forecasting techniques may include linear regression, which is discussed in Section IE11, or simple graphical techniques.

In examining data to make forecasts likely *turning points* are of interest and these may be inferred from *leading indicators* such as orders for durable goods, housing construction or movements in the currencies of other countries when a historical tendency to follow them is known to exist.

2. International Economics

Policy rules

If the monetary policy approach us used, however, simple rules such as

1. Increase money supply (M_1 or M_2) by 4 to 5% per annum.
2. Balance a full employment budget each year.

are all that may be required according to the monetarists.

Such an approach involves no real government decision or action and supposedly permits a much freer market economy. It seems rather optimistic, however, to assume that such simple rules can be put in place and that the system will then run itself without interference. After all, even where there is minimal government interference, wars, plagues, famine or commodity crises may still require policy alteration.

Conclusion

Whatever approach, be it Keynesian (fiscal) or monetary, or a combination of these, the following points should be noted in connection with its implementation:

1. Smoothing of economic behaviour should be done by prompt action in line with policy.
2. Abrupt changes in policy should be avoided.
3. Policy should be based on long term objectives.

With these precautions, therefore, whichever approach is used the short term disturbances resulting from its implementation will be minimized.

IE9. Exchange rates

Currency exchange rates, of course, are an important factor in macroeconomics and not only affect importers and exporters but, in turn, the whole national economy as well. Indeed they also have direct effects, for example upon the stock market and interest rates. In the present section we briefly discuss the foreign exchange market and the exchange rate system.

2. International Economics

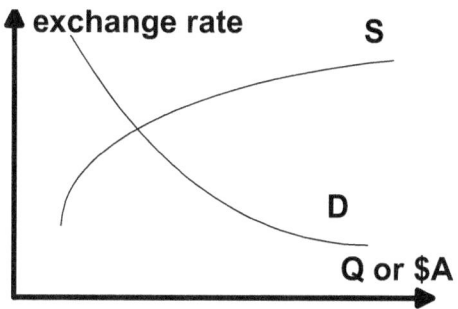

Fig. IE10. S & D curves for the Australian dollar.

Figure IE10 shows hypothetical supply and demand curves for the Australian dollar. These are part of a foreign exchange market which may be likened to a stock market so that the price or exchange rate of the $A is governed by the demand for it and the supply of it.

Such demand is caused when overseas companies buy Australian goods or assets or overseas tourists spend in Australia. On the other hand Australians touring overseas, for example, add to the supply of $As by their spending. This then, is the market mechanism by which exchange rates are now flexible and able to fluctuate daily.

Such fluctuations, however, are able to be limited to some extent by the reserve bank which holds *foreign exchange reserves* of other currencies and can use these to intervene in the market.

For economies highly dependent upon exporting commodities, it is best to peg the exchange rate (Caves et al., 1990).

For many years, however, China has pegged its exchange rate, much to the detriment of the US and other economies, and during the 2016 US election campaign Donald Trump frequently railed against China for this. This, and a number of other apparent errors in modern economic theory, are dealt with by Mohr in several books, sometimes in chapters entitled *Econobabble* (Mohr, 2012, 2014a, 2017, 2018).

2. INTERNATIONAL ECONOMICS

A brief history of the exchange system

Until the end of the Second World War currencies were based on the *gold standard* which equated each unit of a given currency to a certain number of ounces of gold. The gold standard was, in fact, introduced by Isaac Newton in 1717 as one of his first acts as treasurer of the Royal Mint.

During the Great Depression of the 1930s, however, countries began to abandon the gold standard system. In 1945, therefore, the Bretton-Woods system (named after the town in New Hampshire where representatives of the Allies met in 1944 to establish a new system) of foreign exchange was established. In this the *par value* of a currency was stated in gold or $US and values were *pegged* by each individual government.

Then, however, when currencies were *devalued* or *revalued* excessive trade in currency or speculation tended to occur.

Countries were required to maintain a reserve deposit with the *International Monetary Fund* as well as maintain sufficient *international liquidity* by holding reserves in cash and gold. The USA, however, was required to hold its entire reserves in gold and was faced with propping up the IMF system, making it impossible to deal with its own deficits.

Hence the IMF/Bretton Woods system began to break down in 1971 and in 1973 a system of flexible exchange rates was established. This allows countries to concentrate on budgeting for full employment and stable prices without being preoccupied by the balance of payments ($X - M$). In the latter regard it was no longer necessary to decide where to 'peg' a currency and the foreign exchange market of *floating* currencies automatically adjusted itself.

Figure IE11 shows variations in the valuation of three other currencies against the Australian dollar over nearly a decade. This is given to simply illustrate the short term fluctuations but the long term trend should also be noticed.

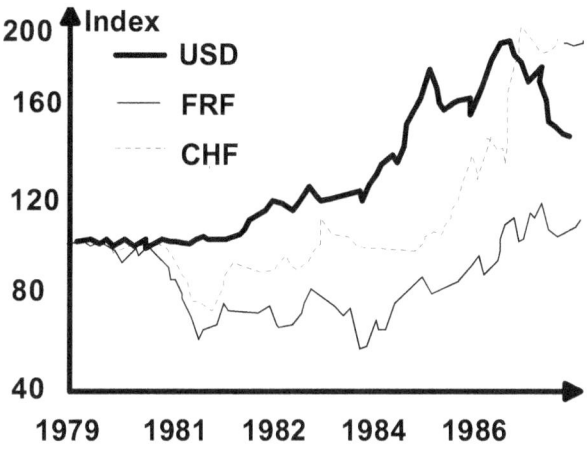

Fig. IE11. Fluctuations against $A

For small open countries, especially those heavily dependent on commodity prices, the advantages of a pegged exchange rate are particularly great, and the great depreciation of the Australian currency since 1970 might remind us of this.

Conclusion

The foreign exchange, like any other market, is subject to supply and demand pressures. The resulting rate variations is one of many factors which complicate international trade, others including tariffs and quotas.

As elsewhere, however, there is a general trend towards reducing such restrictions and freeing up markets. As with most aspects of the economic system, however, we cannot be certain that there will not be some degree of reversal in such trends in the future.

IE10. Socialist systems

In a chapter on macroeconomics entitled International Economics it is perhaps appropriate to briefly discuss socialist systems as these have had a major influence in the USSR and Yugoslavia, for example, and still continue to do so elsewhere. It is also of interest, therefore, to briefly discuss the history of the *Westminster system* of government upon which government in much of the 'west' is based.

What is Socialism?

It is important at the outset to note that *socialism* refers to the 'means of production' being owned by the state whereas *communism* refers to the means of production being owned by the people. The two terms are often confused but in a complex and highly technological modern society it is doubtful that communism is practical. It is doubtful, for example, that the very large companies required in some industries, many of these now multinational ones, can be owned and run by the 'people', taking people to mean those in a particular community.

What is clear, however, is that the Marx-Engels manifesto was anti-capitalist and this was the real spirit of the 1917 Russian revolution, a spirit which many believed would eventually spread globally. This revolution created a socialist state with a long term view towards forming a communist society.

Marx v. the Critics

Marxists will argue that the capitalist *class* accumulates increasingly more capital or a 'surplus value' in fact created by the workers. The working class, therefore, are left to accumulate misery, that is *"In proportion as capital accumulates, the lot of the labourer be his payment high or low, must grow worse"* as Karl Marx put it.

Critics of this view will point out that in practice state ownership leads to totalitarian government which makes the people worse off, rather than better.

2. INTERNATIONAL ECONOMICS

Marxists will also argue that in capitalism monopolies or oligopolies must eventually develop, in turn influencing the political system so that something akin to totalitarianism can result.

In defence against this view critics of Marxism will argue that it is better to reform the capitalist system, not replace it, for example by introducing anti-monopoly laws.

The USSR System

Though the USSR has been more or less dismantled, some aspects of its system remain whilst socialist systems operate elsewhere in the world. Moreover, the communist party in Russia, for example, still has a good deal of support. Hence some discussion of the USSR system as it was is still worthwhile, principal features of that system being:

1. In the USSR policy was based on five year plans. Critics would argue that this was too inflexible and did not allow for adjustments.

2. Without a free market coordination was difficult. Supposing we wished to increase steel production, for example, then we needed extra plant to make it and in turn extra steel to make the plant. In other words it is difficult to be self sufficient as a single entity despite a perhaps massive size.

3. In the USSR investment (I) ran at about 30% of GNP (about the same figure as Japan at the time and twice that for the USA), this funded by a 30% general sales tax (GST).

4. This high level of investment was aimed at building industry but resulted in excessive restrictions in consumption and chronic shortages in goods.

5. In the USSR system there was effectively no such thing as unemployment as everyone could be given a job, however unproductive.

2. INTERNATIONAL ECONOMICS

The Westminster system

A brief history of the Westminster system is:
1. Pre 1066 (Saxon times). The barons and King met each year at Easter, Whitsun and Christmas.
2. 1258 (in the reign of Henry III). A meeting of the barons of England at Oxford was the origin of the *House of Lords*.
3. 1264. Simon de Montfort, on the King's behalf, organized a meeting of two knights from each county.
4. 1265. Two citizens from each county were included in the latter meeting, constituting the origin of the *House of Commons*.
5. In the reign of Elizabeth I the puritans became the first party and were the opposition to the crown.
6. In the reign of James I the cavaliers and roundheads emerged as two opposing political forces.
7. 1681. The origin of the names *Whig* and *Tory*.

What of the future?

Not long ago some economics texts asked the question about socialism and capitalism: "Are the systems converging?"

About the USSR, at least, it is now safe to say that its system has changed and some aspects of socialism, such as centralization of power, have been much reduced. Before the USSR was dismantled, however, there had long been changes such as a greater tendency to pay highly skilled workers more, less interventionist government and slow opening up to outside (and hence not state) capital.

About the future in the USSR, or China, for example, it therefore seems safe to say that there has been a move in the direction of capitalism (and democracy, but this is not necessarily synonymous with any particular economic system).

What can we say about the USA and like countries?

Clearly there is some disenchantment with the two party system. This has been around for 20 to 30 years but may begin to crystallize somewhere.

2. INTERNATIONAL ECONOMICS

In Australia, for example, minor parties and independents often hold the balance of power in the upper house or senate but has no influence in the legislative lower house. In the USA, on the other hand, it is not impossible to imagine a (rich) independent being elected president.

And finally, what can we say about China? What influence will such a potentially powerful country have in the future? Presumably it will increasingly join the global economy and consequently move a little to the right politically.

Conclusion

The politico-economic systems of both the 'east' and the 'west' will doubtless continue to change slowly. Whilst current trends are towards freer capitalist markets it is possible that this trend may be slightly reversed at some point.

IE11. Econometrics

Econometrics is the estimation and refinement of *a priori* relationships between economic quantities. As an example suppose we wish to represent the quantity of a product demanded at time *t* as

(IE13) $\qquad q(t) = a + bp(t) + ci(t) + d(t)$

where $\quad p(t)$ = price function (for product)
$\quad\quad\quad\;\; i(t)$ = income function (for consumers)
$\quad\quad\quad\;\; d(t)$ = disturbance or error function

and *a, b* and *c* are parameters and in this case we expect $b < 0$ and $c > 0$.

Then we use observed data and such techniques as linear regression to determine the values of the parameters *a, b* and c which most closely fit the function *q(t)* to the observed values of demand at various times.

Armed with this result we are than able to use the model of Equation IE13 to *forecast* demand when such estimates are required.

2. INTERNATIONAL ECONOMICS

Linear regression

Linear regression fits a line of 'best fit' to observed data on a *least squares basis* (usually), that is we minimize the sum

$$\Sigma \text{ distance(points - regression line)}^2$$

For example, suppose we are given two sets of marks for students, x and y, respectively expected (from previous results) and actual results for a test. Then these marks are shown in the first two columns of Table IE2, followed by two further columns obtained from them which are used to allow quick calculation of the required line.

As shown, the sum of each column is obtained, the first two summed giving

$$x_{av} = \Sigma\, x/N = 36/7 \text{ and } y_{av} = \Sigma\, y/N = 6$$

Table IE2.

	x	y	x^2	xy
	8	10	64	80
	7	8	49	56
	3	2	9	6
	5	6	25	30
	7	9	49	63
	2	2	4	4
	4	5	16	20
S	36	42	216	259

Then the slope of the line

(IE14) $\qquad y = y_{av} + b(x - x_{av})$

is given by

$b = \{NSxy - SxSy\}/\{NSx^2 - (Sx)^2\} = \{7(259) - 36(42)\}/\{7(216) - 1296\} = 1.39$

so that the required line is

$$y = 6 + 1.39(x - 5.14)$$

Then when we want to establish whether such data fits a parabola, for example, we should seek a regression line for x v. $y/x = y^*$ in the same manner, replacing y by y^* above.

Conclusion

Linear regression is a simple matter, as the example of Table IE2 shows. It is customary to use a least squares basis but, for example, a linear basis would simply involve a third column:

$$(y - y_{av})/(x - x_{av}) = \delta y/\delta x$$

and dividing the sum of this column by N we obtain an estimate of b (where δy or $\delta x = 0$ such points are ignored and N reduced by one). A least squares basis, however, is more accurate and no more difficult to use.

References

Aarons, R. and Loftus, A. *The Secret War Against the Jews*, Mandarin Press, Melbourne, 1999.

Attiyek, R., Lumsden, K. and Bach, G.L. *Macroeconomics: A Programmed Book*, 2nd edn., Prentice-Hall, Englewood Cliffs NJ, 1970.

_____. *Transcripts on the Poltical Economy of Development.* Australian Broadcasting Commission, Sydney. 1977

Benham, F. *Economics*, 6th edn. Pitman, London, 1960.

Black, E. *IBM and the Holocaust.* Little Brown, London, 2001.

Booker, M. *The Last Domino: Aspects of Australia's Foreign Relations.* Sun Books, Melbourne, 1978.

Caves, RE, Frankel, JA, Jone, RW, *World Trade and Payments, An Introduction*, 5th edn. Scott, Foresman/Little, Brown, Glenview IL, 1990,

Crough, G., Wheelwright, T. and Wiltshire, T. *Australia and World Capitalism.* Penguin, Ringwood VIC, 1980.

David, A., Wheelwright, T. *The Third Wave.* Left Book Club Co-op. Ltd, Sydney, 1989.

Gilpin, R. *War and Change in World Politics.* CUP, Cambridge, 1981.

2. INTERNATIONAL ECONOMICS

Gilpin, R. *The Political Economy of International Relations.* Princeton Univ. Press, Princeton NJ. 1987.

Hunt, E.K. and Sherman, H.J. *Economics: An Introduction to Traditional and Radical Views,* 4th edn. Harper & Row, New York. 1981.

Jay, P. *The Crisis of Western Political Economy.* Australian Broadcasting Commission, Sydney, 1980.

L.R. Klein, *Economic Fluctuations in The United States, 1921-1941*, John Wiley & Sons, New York, 1950.

Klein, L.R., Pauly, P. and Voison, P. The world economy - a global model. *Perspectives in Computing*, vol. 2, no. 2, 1982.

Levinson, M. Capitalism with a safety net? *Harvard Business Review,* Sept-Oct. 1996.

Leontief, W.W. *The Structure of the American Economy, 1919-1939*, 2nd edn. OUP, Fair Lawn NJ. 1951.

Lindert, P.H. *Prices, Jobs and Growth: an Introduction to Macroeconomics.* Little Brown, Boston MA, 1976.

MacKenzie, K. *The English Parliament.* Pelican, Harmondsworth, 1963.

Mintzberg, H. Managing government, governing management. *Harvard Business Review*, May-June 1996.

Mohr, G.A. Time Stepping of Macroeconomic Models. *Appl. Maths Comput.*, Vol. 102, pp 273-278, 1999.

Mohr GA, *The Doomsday Calculation,* Xlibris, Sydney, 2012.

Mohr GA, *The Pretentious Persuaders,* 2nd edn, Horizon Publishing Group, 2014a.

Mohr G.A., *Elementary Thinking for the 21st Century*, Xlibris, Sydney, 2014b.

Mohr GA, *The Scientific MBA,* 5th edn, Balboa Press, Bloomingon, Indiana, 2017.

2. International Economics

Mohr GA, *Elementary Thinking for Modern Management,* Amazon-Kindle, 2018.

Mohr GA, Mohr RS, Mohr PE, *The Population Explosion,* Amazon-Kindle, 2018.

Sampson. *The Arms Bazaar.* Coronet, Sevenoaks, Kent, 1977.

Shavelson, R.J. *Statistical Reasoning for the Behavioural Sciences*, 2nd edn. Allyn & Bacon, Boston MA, 1976.

Smith, A. *Paper Money.* Summit Books, New York NY. 1981.

Sweezy, P.M. *The Theory of Capitalist Development*. Dennis Dobson, London, 1946.

Tarshis, L. Modern Economics. Houghton Mifflin, Boston. 1967.

Vernon, J. *Macroeconomics.* Dryden Press, Hinsdale IL, 1980.

Wells, S.J. *International Economics.* Allen & Unwin, London, 1969.

Wonnacott, P. and Wonnacott, R. *Economics.* McGraw-Hill, New York, 1979 + Howitt, P. *Study Guide to Accompany Wonnaccott/Wonnacott: Economics.* McGraw-Hill, New York, 1979.

2. International Economics

Chapter 3

MICROECONOMICS (ME)

> *Economics is as much a study in fantasy and aspirations as in hard numbers - maybe more so.*
> Theodore Roszak, *The Making of a Counter Culture* (1975).

The preceding chapter discussed macroeconomics, that is, national and international economic matters such as the foreign exchange market. In this chapter *microeconomics* is discussed, that is, economic management of the local market and corporations, sometimes referred to as managerial economics.

ME1. Elasticity

In the preceding chapter we introduced the concept of supply and demand and the associated S & D curves were much used to explain economic phenomena. By consideration of the *elasticity* of supply and demand many more useful applications of the theory of supply and demand are found.

In Equation IE2 we defined elasticity as

(ME1) $\quad e = (\delta Q/Q)/(\delta P/P)$

so that it is the quotient of the fractional or percentage changes in Q and P.

When we are dealing with a curve and $\delta Q = Q_2 - Q_1$, $\delta P = P_2 - P_1$ for two points which values of Q and P should we use in calculating elasticity?

3. MICROECONOMICS

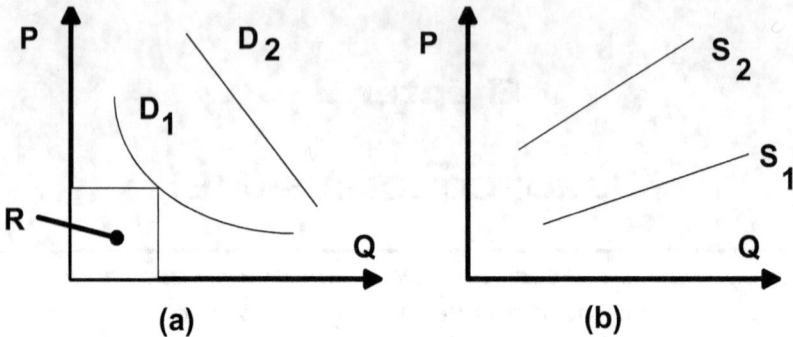

Fig. ME1. Elasticity of supply and demand.

The answer is to define e as:

(ME2) $\quad e = (\delta Q/Q_{av})/(\delta P/P_{av})$

where $Q_{av} = (Q_1 + Q_2)/2$, $P_{av} = (P_1 + P_2)/2$

That is, e is calculated as the *inverse slope of the chord* between the two points on the curve. In the limit, therefore, $e = \delta Q/\delta P$ is the *inverse slope* of the curve at a point.

Figure ME1(a) shows two demand curves:
 (a) D_1 is for *elastic* demand ($e < -1$) and $\delta P \rightarrow -\delta R$
 (b) D_2 is for *inelastic* demand ($e > -1$) and $\delta P \rightarrow +\delta R$
where R is the *revenue* which is given by the shaded area shown in Figure ME1(a) for a given point. Hence when demand is elastic and increase in price gives a decrease in revenue.

Figure ME1(b) shows two supply curves. The curve S_1 is *elastic* ($e > 1$) and hence 'flat' whilst S_2 is *inelastic* ($e < 1$) and 'steep'.

Application of the elasticity concept

Figure ME2(a) shows the effect of an increase in price, for example as the result of imposition of a tax, when demand is elastic (or 'flat'). Then operation moves to point X and the seller bears most of the burden of the price increase, as shown.

3. Microeconomics

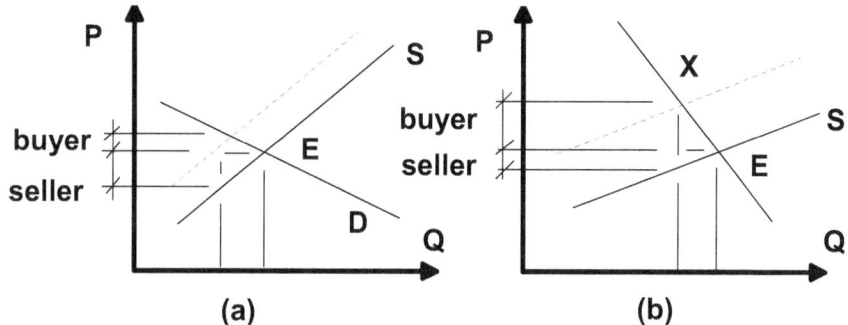

Fig. ME2. Price changes with (a) elastic D, (b) elastic S.

When the supply is elastic, on the other hand, the buyer bears most of the price increase, as shown in Figure ME2(b).

Clearly, therefore, elasticity is very important in considering the effect of price increases as the effects on revenue and whether the sellers of buyers bear the burden of such increases depends upon the elasticity of supply or demands.

Factors in elasticity of demands

Examples of factors which affect elasticity of demand include:

1. Luxury items (for example hats) tend to have elastic demand whereas essentials (such as electricity) have inelastic demand.
2. Cost and hence proportion of available funds is an important factor and, for example, expensive items such as cars have elastic demand while cheap (and perhaps essential) items such as toothpaste have inelastic demand.
3. Availability of alternatives is another factor. When alternative products exist, for example competing types of confectionary, demand is elastic but when there are almost no alternatives (for example salt) demand is inelastic.
4. Whether items are required immediately or for use in the long term is another key factor. Ski equipment, for example, will tend to have elastic demand whereas items like car parts have inelastic demand.

3. MICROECONOMICS

Factors in elasticity of supply

Similarly there are many simple factors which affect the elasticity of supply, examples being the following:

1. Products with low storage cost will tend to have elastic supply whereas those for which storage cost is high, for example food, will have inelastic supply.
2. Products for which storage is of limited feasibility, such as perishable goods, will have inelastic supply whilst goods which have no such constraints will have elastic supply.
3. When substitute products can be produced when necessary, for example substitute crops for farming, then supply is elastic but when substitution is not possible supply is inelastic.
4. When goods must be disposed of in the short term (for example perishable or other goods with a limited shelf life) then supply is inelastic whereas where goods need only be sold in the long term then supply is elastic.

Special problems of agriculture

Discussion of factors affecting elasticity of supply and demand has already considered problems such as those of perishable goods and the essential nature of food products. Other special problems of agriculture include:

1. Seasonal fluctuations in supply.

2. Boom crops which shift the supply curve S to the right in Fig. ME2(b) and thus cause a drop in price.

3. Droughts which have the opposite result of (2), that is, a shortage occurs along with an increase in price.

4. 'Food mountains' stored over years to maintain prices are then difficult to dispose of.

5. Global surpluses can lead to a local surplus being exacerbated.

In general, indeed, agriculture is more prone to fluctuations in supply and demand and it is often difficult to cope with the problems that result.

3. Microeconomics

Conclusion

The degree of elasticity of supply and demand curves has an important influence on the effect of changes in supply and demand. There are many factors which determine whether supply or demand is elastic or inelastic. Both supply and demand of agriculture products, however, tend to be inelastic and agriculture has many special problems as a result.

ME2. Demand and Supply Variations

In the following section we introduce the concept of *utility* and then of *marginal* utility and cost. These are very important quantities used in determining quantities of goods to supply.

Marginal utility

We define utility as the satisfaction a customer gains from buying a unit of a particular product. Then the *marginal utility* is the satisfaction from buying one additional unit. Expressing this in dollars and assuming that satisfaction (or usefulness, and hence price the buyer is prepared to pay) decreases with each further unit bought, that is the 'law of diminishing utility', the result being equivalent to a demand curve.

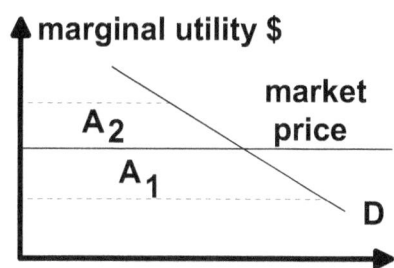

Fig. ME3. Consumer surplus.

Figure ME3 shows an example in which D is the utility function for a buyer. If the market price is as shown then the area A_2 represents purchase at utility exceeding market price and is the *consumer surplus*. When utility is less than purchase price, however, the consumer surplus represented by area A_1 is negative.

3. MICROECONOMICS

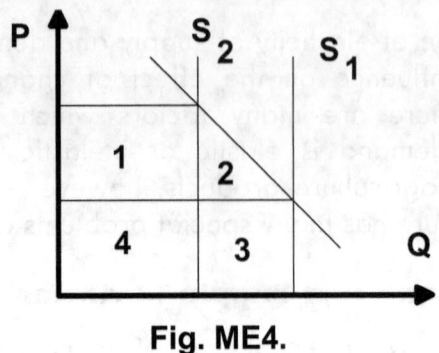

Fig. ME4.

Figure ME4 shows an example of this surplus concept. Suppose there is a drought and the (inelastic) supply of an agricultural product drops from S_1 to S_2. Then the areas 1 and 2 represent a negative consumer surplus or consumer deficit. Similarly area 3 is a negative producer surplus (producer surplus is discussed at the end of this section).

Then the losses and gains may be summarized as follows:

Consumers	lose 1	lose 2
Producers	gain 1	lose 3
Σ = nation		lose 2 lose 3

leading to the conclusion that as a result of the price rising the consumers lose (as expected), whereas the producers might with a little luck gain a little but the nation as a while loses in terms of lost GNP.

The marginal cost (MC) or producing an item is the increase in total cost involved in producing one additional item.

Figure ME5 shows a typical example where marginal cost increases as Q increases (that is, the 'law of diminishing returns').

3. Microeconomics

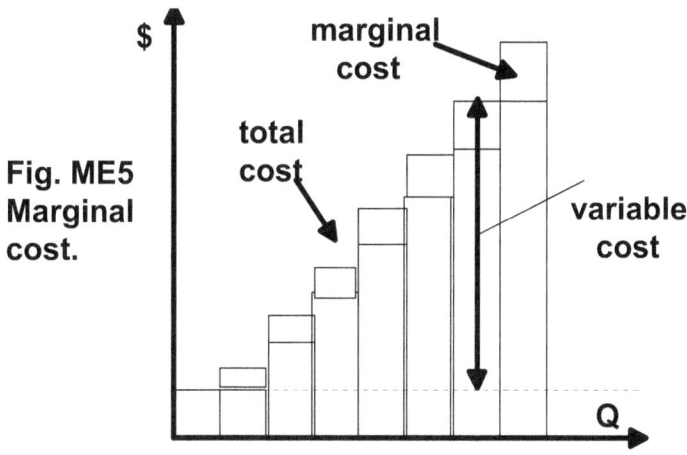

Fig. ME5 Marginal cost.

This increasing marginal cost is shown in Figure ME6 where the point of intersection with the marginal return (MR), here a constant price, gives the optimum production quantity and the maximum profit (see Section IE2).

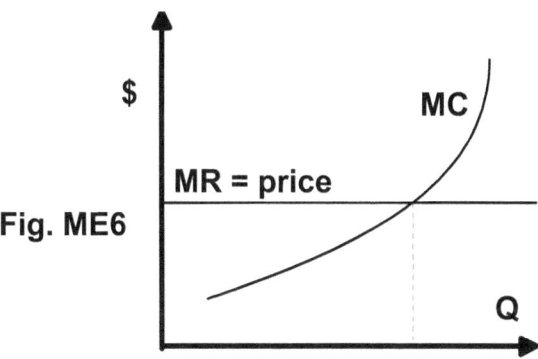

Fig. ME6

Short run supply curve

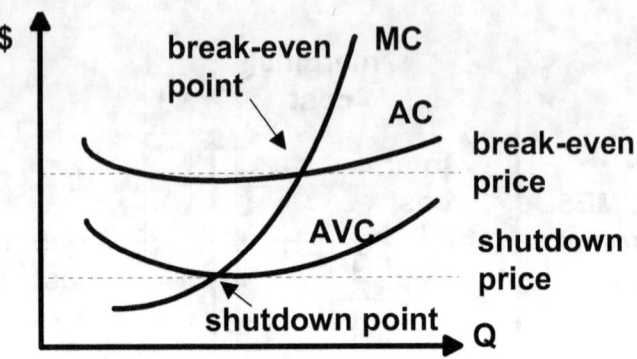

Fig. ME7. Short run supply curve.

If we define average cost as total cost divided by output and average variable cost as total variable cost divided by output the curves AC and AVC are obtained in Figure ME7.

Then the MC curve intersects the AVC cost at the *shutdown point* and output Q below this level does not cover variable costs (or fixed costs) and the short run supply curve is the portion of the MC curve above this point.

The MC curve then intersect the AC curve at its minimum (because to the left of the intersection point MC < AC and MC 'pulls the AC curve down' and to the right MC > AC and MC 'pushes the AC curve up') and this is the *break-even* price and output at above this level is profitable.

Example.

As a simple example, suppose you own a second house for which the fixed costs of your mortgage etc. are $200 pw and the variable costs are $40 pw, whereas you rent it for only $100 pw. Should you keep renting it?

The answer is yes in the short term as this will at least help cover your costs. At least until you can sell it, that is, which is what you should do in the long term unless considerable capital gains are expected.

Long run supply curve

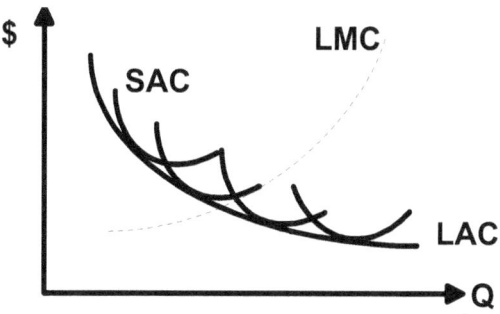

Fig. ME8. Long run supply curve

The short run supply curve deals with a particular 'level' or 'range' of operation. When there are several different ranges, for example corresponding to several factories or production lines (some of which can be shut down), we draw short run average cost curves (SAC) for each level of operation as shown in Figure ME8.

Then the locus of these is the long run average cost curve (LAC) and this intersects the long run marginal cost curve (LAC) at the *long run breakeven point* and the *long run supply curve* is the part of the LMC curve above this point.

Producer surplus

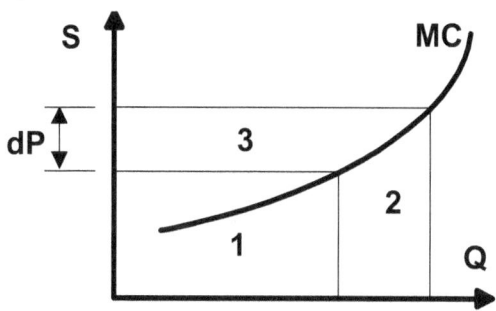

Fig. ME9. Consumer surplus

Fig.ure ME9 shows the MC curve for a producer. If there is a price increase *dP*, as shown, then areas 2 + 3 give the increase in revenue, area 2 being a cost so that area 3 is the *producer surplus*.

3. Microeconomics

Conclusion

Marginal utility/cost curves are equivalent to supply and demand curves and once again such curves are shown to have very useful applications in illustrating the effects of price changes and critical points such as break-even points in cost-quantity studies.

ME3. Competition and Monopoly

In assuming demand and supply curves to this point we have assumed a perfectly competitive market, that is, the prices are determined by market forces and not by arbitrary means. In the following section we discuss the notion of a competitive market and associated problems.

Perfect competition

In a (perfectly) competitive market it is assumed that:
1. Social benefit = private benefit, so that marginal benefit of a product to society = marginal utility (to the user), i.e. MU.
2. Social cost = private cost, so that marginal cost of a product to society = marginal cost (of production), i.e. MC.

Then in a competitive market:
consumers purchase until   MU = P
companies produce until   P = MC
so that   MU = MC

and this result applies to both private and public production and consumption.

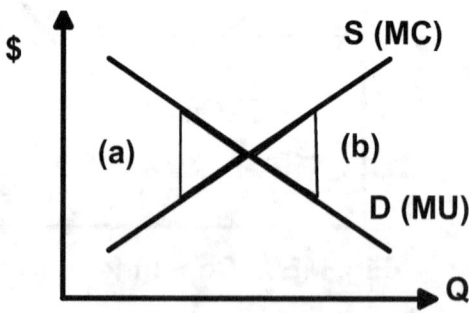

Fig. ME 10. Efficiency losses.

3. Microeconomics

When production is at levels other than for MU = PC there are efficiency losses such as that shown by the shaded areas in Figure ME10. In case (a) fewer potentially beneficial units are produced than required and in case (b) each unit produced has MC > MU.

Markets, of course, are not perfect and are affected by such things as:

a. Distribution of income, the demand curves of different individuals depending on their income.

b. Market information will be unequal and sometimes misleading.

c. Speculative buying (for resale, not consumption).

d. Government subsidies (which considerably affect agricultural supply, for example).

e. Monopolies, cartels etc.

Discussion of the latter, the other points being discussed at other points in the text, follows in the remainder of this section.

Monopoly

Monopolies arise in such situations as the following:

1. A company has control over an input or technique required to make a product.

2. Through the law, for example where postal services are run by government or bus services are given exclusive contracts to operate routes.

3. Natural monopoly, that is, where no other company can match the cost efficiencies of an established company.

4. Collusion, for example where two or more companies form a cartel.

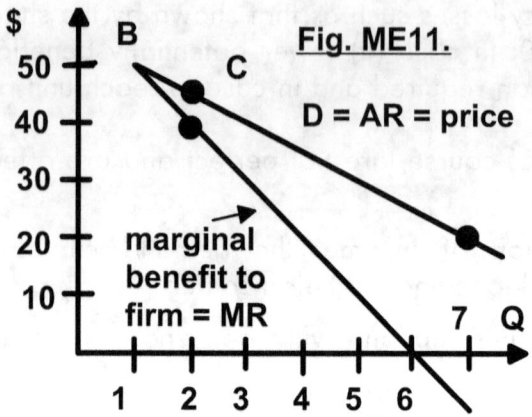

Fig. ME11.

Fig.ure ME11 shows the demand (= average revenue) curve for a monopoly. If we move from point B at which 1 unit was sold for $50 to point C were 2 units are sold for $45 the marginal revenue for the firm

$$= 2(45) - 50 = \$40$$

Continuing such calculation for the full range of Figure ME11 the results shown in Table ME1 are obtained.

Hence for a monopoly the MR and D curves differ and MR < P (price). This has followed from the assumption that D = AR = price. This is so for monopolies because the demand for a single firm is the market demand.

Table ME1. Derivation of MR for Figure ME11

Q	P = AR	P x Q	MR
1	50	50	50
2	45	90	40
3	40	120	30
4	35	140	20
5	30	150	10
6	25	150	0
7	20	140	-10

Monopoly output and price

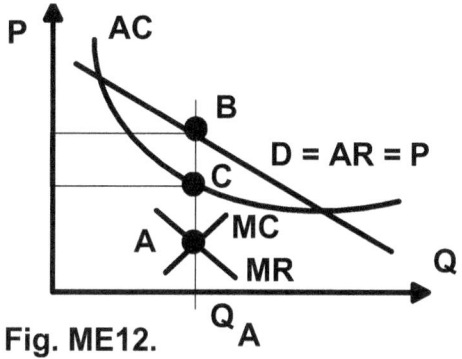

Fig. ME12.
Equilibrium of a monopoly

In Figure ME6 it is shown that efficient operation is at the intersection of marginal cost and marginal utility or benefit. For a monopoly MU = MR so that point A in Figure ME12 is chosen, giving output Q_A.

Then the price to sell at follows from the demand (= AR = P) curve, giving point B which is referred to as the profit-maximizing point on the demand curve.

This profit = Q_A × BC = shaded area in Figure ME12.

Conclusion

Monopolies involve the following disadvantages:

1. Prices are greater than they would be in a competitive market.

2. Production will tend to be less than in a competitive market.

3. They tend to be inefficient as their 'price freedom' allows this.

Hence antimonopoly policies and legislation are common along with price regulation and auditing to alleviate such difficulties.

3. Microeconomics

ME4. Oligopoly

Oligopoly is domination of a market by a few companies. The degree to which this occurs is measured by the *concentration ratio,* that is, the proportion of the market that is captured by (say) four companies. The most obvious example is the car industry but others occur in the packaged food industry, for example.

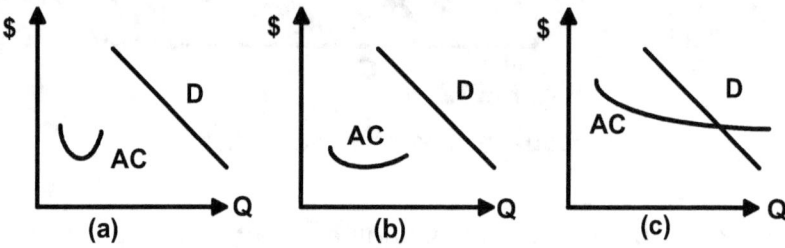

Fig. ME13. Perfect market, oligopoly and monopoly.

Figure ME13(a) illustrates the situation in a competitive market. Here the 'cost range' of a firm is such that many firms are needed to supply the market. Many agricultural products are examples of this situation.

Figure ME13(b) illustrated the situation of *natural oligopoly,* that is where the AC curves of individual firms fall over a large range so that only a few firms are needed to meet demand.

Natural oligopoly often occurs as a result of economies of scale in certain industries such as the car industry where mass production is particularly beneficial in reducing cost.

Figure ME13(c) illustrates the situation of *natural monopoly,* that is where the AC curve for a single firm may only bottom close to the demand curve or even after it. An example is the steel industry.

Companies of case (b) are not required to expand by market forces but may seek *market power,* leading to movement towards monopoly. Alternatively, oligopoly companies may collude to fix prices, for example the OPEC cartel and its actions in the 1970s.

Bilinear demand

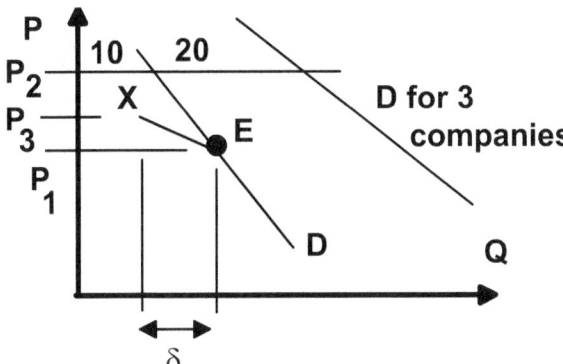

Fig. ME14. Bilinear demand function

Figure ME14 shows the demand curve for a company which is one of three forming an oligopoly, each having an equal market share of 10 units. The company is operating at point E but wishes to increase price to P_2.

If, however, the competitors hold their prices the company will lose market share by the amount δ shown and will be forced to sell at price P_3 to maintain this reduced market share, so that the actual demand function takes the bilinear form shown (i.e. D-E-X).

Non-price competition

Not all competition in markets is simply by way of price, which has dominated the discussion to this point. Companies may also compete, of course, by advertising etc. or through research and development to refine products and production. When very large amounts are spend on such activities over a long period it can form a *barrier* to new entrants to the market.

Conclusion

Oligopoly occurs naturally when economies of scale favour it and then it offers a price advantage to the consumer. It also has the advantage of often involving large research and development budgets which lead to product improvements and development of new products, thus giving additional benefit to consumers and to industry.

ME5. External Costs and Benefits

In recent decades we have become increasingly aware of external costs which result from production such as pollution (requiring prevention and/or clean up costs) and congestion (freeways and high rise buildings are more costly than their counterparts on a 'unit usage' basis). Equally, it is important to realize that some public services provide external benefits, that is, benefits to certain people regardless of who paid for them.

Pollution

Pollution of the air, water, or noise pollution involve two types of costs, namely
1. *Internal costs* of prevention, cleanup etc.
2. *External costs* (or downstream costs) of cleanup, damage repair, compensation etc.

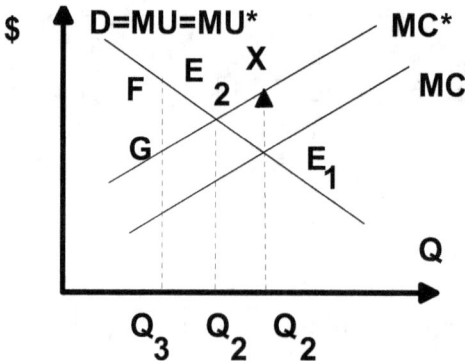

Fig. ME15. External costs or limits

Suppose a free market is operating in equilibrium at point E_1 with output Q_1 and that a tax is implemented to provide for the costs of pollution cleanup forcing operation to move to point E_2 on the MC* curve which is the marginal cost curve for society. Then in relation to MC* (and not MC) there is an efficiency gain $= E_1XE_2$.

If, however, there was, in addition, a production limit Q_3 imposed to limit pollution there would be an efficiency loss E_2FG.

3. Microeconomics

If allowance for cleanup costs is included in determination of economic formulation of operating points and allowance made for social costs then from the broader point of view optimum production is possible.

Recycling

Recycling, as well as cleanup, reduces pollution and can be allowed for in budgeting. In addition recycling reduces consumption, of course, so that it provides two benefits.

Congestion

Traffic congestion can be reduced by, for example, small tolls which act like the tax in Fig. ME15 and will reduce peak flows and in turn reduce the need for further freeway construction.

In some cases lower public transport fares in peak periods can actually prove more economical, the increased revenue reducing the deficit caused by unprofitable off peak services. This in turn reduces traffic congestion.

Price, of course, need not be the only incentive for public transport. Provision of bus only lanes and the like can give public transport a comparative advantage in congested areas.

Public services

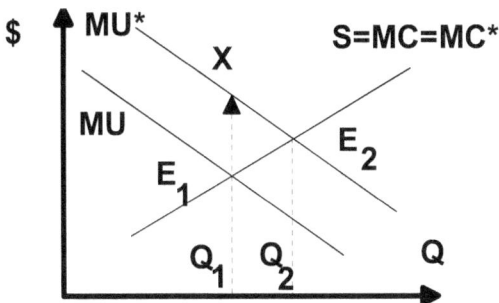

Fig. ME16. Efficiency gain with a public service.

Suppose a free market is operating at equilibrium at point E_1 with output Q_1 in Figure ME16, but the product involved has a 'general social benefit', that is the community at large as well as the customers.

3. Microeconomics

Then when this social benefit is taken into account the marginal utility curve is MU*. Then, if a subsidy is paid by the government to move output to level Q_2, and hence operation to point E_2, there is an efficiency gain (in relation to MU*) of E_1E_2X.

Once again, therefore, we see how allowance for social factors in utility (or return) and cost can lead to rational economic models which, in relation to these factors are efficient.

Benefit-cost analysis

Benefit-cost analysis is a well known technique in which simple tables of costs and benefits of alternative schemes are used to determine preferred plans for public works, choosing first those projects which have the largest *benefit-cost ratio*.

Such techniques can readily include social factors in their benefit calculations whilst demand and supply and marginal utility and cost information can provide data for their application.

Conclusion

Pollution and public services have been used respectively as examples of the use of adjusted marginal cost and utility functions, interpreting these as examples of social cost or benefit. The adjustments used here to allow for tax (or price) and quota impositions can, of course, be used in any context.

ME6. International Trade

Some of the advantages of international trade to local markets include:

1. It provides increased competition.
2. Economies of scale are encouraged locally in order to compete with overseas markets.
3. It introduces foreign industries with 'comparative advantage' which can produce at lower 'opportunity cost' (see Section IE1) into the local market, in turn encouraging local producers with such advantage to export.
4. Technological change is often introduced, boosting local production and in turn overall international trade.

3. MICROECONOMICS

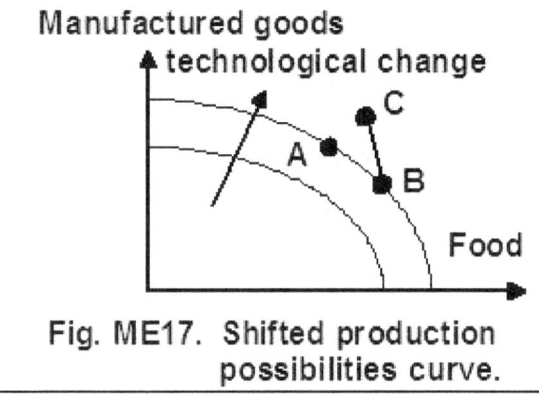

Fig. ME17. Shifted production possibilities curve.

Figure ME17 shows an example of the effect of technological change introduced by international trade. Here new technology shifts the production possibilities curve (PPC, see Section IE1) outwards so that total production and consumption may be increased.

Then the effect of specialization can also be shown by, for example, an increase in food production in moving from point A to B. Then through international trade the shortfall in production of manufactured goods is made up by moving from point B to C, beyond the PPC curve and yielding greater total production and consumption than would be possible in the local market.

Effect of imports and exports on costs and production

Figure ME18 illustrates the effect of exports. Here there is a fall in local consumption $Q_0 - Q_1$ but an increase in production $Q_2 - Q_0$ to provide the required exports. With the fall in local consumption there is an increase in demand and price rises to P_e.

Then the efficiency gain of these changes resulting from exports is the sum of areas 3 and 4 in Figure ME18.

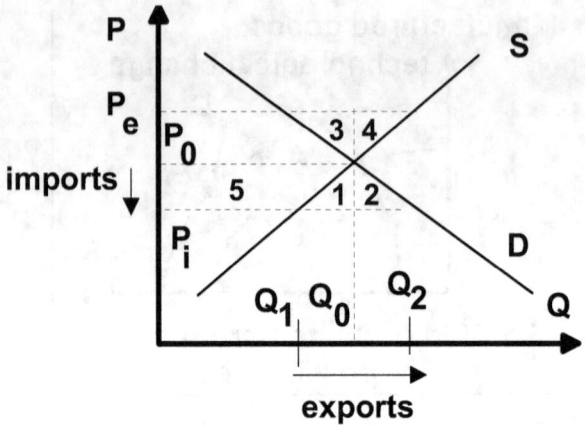

Fig. ME18. Effects of imports & exports

With imports, on the other hand, price decreases to P_i and there is a decrease in local production $Q_0 - Q_1$, and there is an increase in consumption $Q_2 - Q_0$.

Hence the producers lose the revenue of area 5 but the consumers gain an increase in consumption and corresponding benefit equal to areas 5 + 1+ 2. Thus there is an overall efficiency gain of areas 1 + 2 transferred from the producers to the consumers.

Note, however, that in the case of imports we might be concerned about loss of employment resulting from the decrease in local production. As a result of the fall in prices, though, there may be an overall increase in real income.

The effects of tariffs etc.

The effects of tariffs, quotas, subsidies etc. on local and international trade involve such issues and effects as:
1. Tariffs and other 'protectionist' measures are often deemed necessary in the case of 'essential' industries such as the defence industry.
2. Such protection may be used to maintain employment levels and in turn is sometimes an issue of 'electoral sensitivity' so that timing of protection measures may not be desirable from the economic point of view.

3. Microeconomics

3. Advertising campaigns to encourage buying of local products to protect local jobs are common and, indeed, 'buying local' does have this effect.
4. Local industry often campaigns against imports of 'cheap labour' goods.
5. Removal of protection tends to force local prices to match lower import prices.
6. Restriction of trade doesn't result in cheaper imports but may help diversify local trade.
7. Protection may be used to allow development of new industries but the question of how long to maintain it is a difficult one.

Multinational corporations.

Multinational corporations (MNCs) can affect monopoly and even affect government policy in host countries and consequently they are regarded by many as undesirable.

On the other side of this coin, however, the overseas operations of MNCs have the effect of a loss of jobs in the 'home' country (with a flow-on effect to other industries) where their funds could have been invested. There is also a corresponding loss of technology advantage over the host countries.

Trade blocs

Trade blocs such as the EEC have become important players in international trade and their actions can result in price and access barriers to outsiders.

On the other hand such agreements as the GATT (General Agreement on Tariffs and Trade) agreement, first set up in 1947, have had a considerable effect in signatory and other countries in reducing international tariffs.

Conclusion

International trade is generally beneficial and over recent decades there has been a general tendency to reduce tariffs and a movement towards a global market economy. Locally the effects of international trade on employment are still of concern and integrated domestic and international trade policies are needed to alleviate such concerns.

3. MICROECONOMICS

Recently, however, there is an increased interest in developing *regional trade*, that is trade within a 'world region' such as SE Asia where there is an ASEAN treaty, or, or course, Europe. Such trade is a subset of total international trade in which special agreements concerning particular areas of trade are sometimes reached.

Finally, trade agreements are sometimes reached between two neighbouring counties, for example Australia and New Zealand or Canada and the USA and these are another subset of total international trade.

ME7. The Labour Market

We now turn our attention to applying supply and demand considerations to the labour market. Here such considerations as productivity, wage rates, statutory minimum wages and the like can be examined using the concepts of marginal cost and marginal benefit.

Marginal productivity of labour

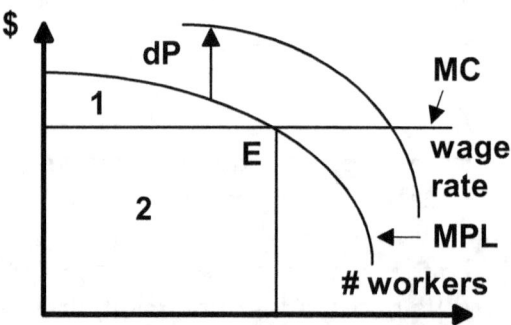

Fig. ME19. Demand for labour.

The marginal physical product of labour is the additional number of units of output a firm can produce when it hires one additional worker. The dollar value of this product is the *marginal productivity of labour (MPL)* and the curve of this is the demand curve for labour, as shown in Figure ME19.

As expected this has a 'diminishing returns' character.

3. Microeconomics

Then the cost of labour is, or course, the wage rate and this is the marginal cost to the firm of employing one more worker. Then the intersection of the MPL and MC curves gives the number of workers required and thus a company should hire until MPL = wage rate.

Then at the equilibrium point E the total labour cost of production is equal to area 2 and area 1 is the cost of other factors of production.

If the product being manufactured increases in price then the MPL curve rises by an amount dP as shown in Figure ME19. Thus the equilibrium point moves to the right and the demand for labour is increased.

Effect of a minimum wage

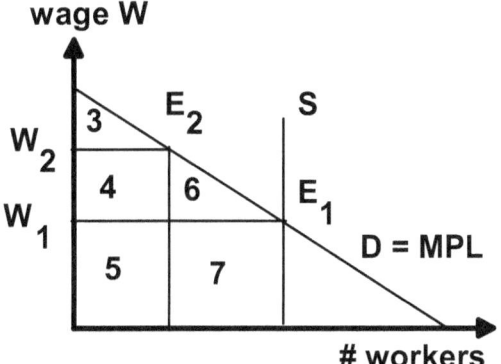

Fig. ME20. Effect of increase in minimum wage.

Figure ME20 shows the effect of increasing a minimum wage form W_1 and W_2, shifting operation from E_1 and E_2 (here assuming that the labour supply curve is a vertical line and hence point E_1 was at full employment).

Then workers still employed gain the revenue of area 4 but those losing their jobs lose the revenue of area 7. Other factors of production lose the revenue of areas 4 and 6. Then the net loss of efficiency is the sum of areas 6 and 7.

3. MICROECONOMICS

Thus the overall effect is a loss of productivity and, of course, wages on the part of those who lose their jobs. Only a minority, therefore, those still employed gain (and consumers lose also from higher prices).

The effect of unions

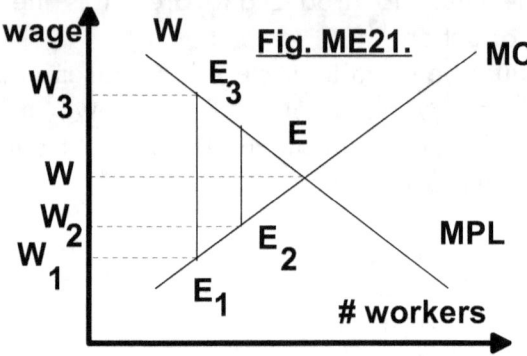

Fig. ME21.

Until now we have considered the case of a perfectly competitive market. Now suppose a *monopsonist* (single buyer) controls the labour market and, when operation is at equilibrium point E, reduces the wage rate to W_1.

Then, as shown in Figure ME21 there is an efficiency loss EE_1E_3. If a union then negotiates a wage W_2 between the two previous rates some of the lost efficiency is regained. But, on the other hand, if the union is able to set a higher wage W_3 the same efficiency loss obtained with wage reduction to W_1 occurs.

In practice, or course, a result between the two extremes is expected as a result of collective bargaining etc.

Industrial action

Industrial action (usually strikes) seeking better wages and conditions may result in a compromise that will suit both parties better in the long term.

Such action can have a flow-on effect to other companies and industries which may be adversely affected (for example an auto workers strike might result in closure of a small parts supplier). Such effects may then rebound on the origin of the action.

Strikes in certain public service areas are electorally sensitive (such as in the health area) and can have wide effects, perhaps impacting other public service areas.

Finally, it should be noted that strikes do not always affect a company as adversely as might be expected. Sometimes, for example, it allows time to run down overstocked inventory. Indeed companies have been known to 'engineer' strikes to this end.

Conclusion

The labour market provides yet another example of supply and demand at work. Here productivity and wage increases are amongst the major considerations and once again S & D curves provide useful insights into the effects of these.

Generally, however, wage increases need to be treated with caution, as Figure ME20 shows, because sometimes only a relatively small number of people stand to gain if heavy job losses result or the rest of the community is affected.

Finally, special situations such as *bilateral monopoly* can occur when an employer has monopoly power and the union has monopoly power. Outcomes may then depend upon the bargaining skills of the parties as well as upon economic considerations.

ME8. Income from capital assets

Around 75% of national income is from wages and salaries. The remainder is made up of income from such assets as capital (debt or equity capital) and property and land. These make up an important part of the overall economic system.

Debt capital

Figure ME22 shows the S & D curves for loan capital, the latter being the *marginal efficiency of investment (MEI)* line, that is another 'law of diminishing returns' type of function. Then operation is at the equilibrium point E shown.

3. MICROECONOMICS

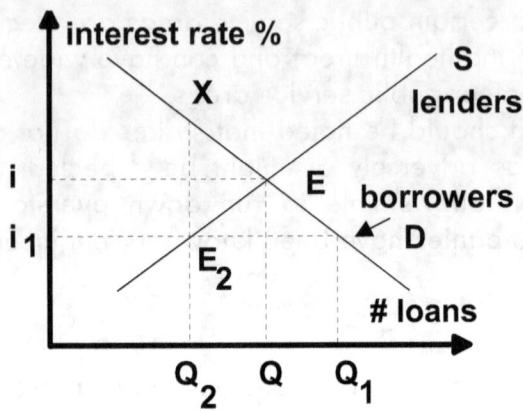

Fig. ME22. Effect of an interest rate ceiling

Then if an interest rate ceiling i_1 is arbitrarily imposed, demand is theoretically Q_1 but supply is limited to Q_2 and thus operation moves to point E_2 and fewer loans are given. There is also a loss of efficiency E_2EX which is transferred from borrowers to lenders (who retain their funds), that is there is a loss of efficient projects etc. which are not funded.

If, on the other hand, the supply of loans was fixed by a vertical line as in Figure ME20, then an entirely different result is obtained and, in fact, there is a loss of efficiency in raising interest rates.

Equity capital

The same arguments for debt capital apply to the supply and demand of equity capital (that is shares in public companies). In addition, rates of return are based on a risk free rate (for the safest stocks) plus a premium based on the market's general rates and a multiplying beta factor for the risk of the individual company and its shares. This is discussed in the first, BF (Business Finance), chapter.

3. MICROECONOMICS

Human capital

Human capital refers to the investment costs of education and training and the value of skills thus acquired.

One of the key questions this raises is who should pay for such training? Generally, in fact, a mixture of payment methods exist and often the employee *contributes* to the costs by direct or deferred payment, employers contribute through taxes and assistance with employee costs, whilst the government provides the initial and major ongoing funding.

Recent trends in this area have seen a narrowing of the salary gap between university and high school graduates in some countries (but a widening in others, particularly in certain specializations) and an increase in private training courses of a relatively short duration along with an increase in 'vocational' training via one or two year courses.

Rent

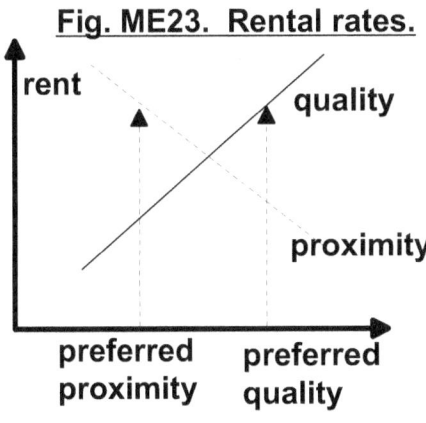

Fig. ME23. Rental rates.

Rental rates depend upon a number of factors. As shown in Fig. ME23, for example, rates may increase with proximity to the CBD of a city (for dwellings and offices, the reverse might be true for farming land).

They may also increase with the 'quality' of the individual area in question (for example its fertility in the case of farming land) and also with the quality of the location or general surrounding area (for example 'posh' suburbs, or course, command a higher rental).

3. Microeconomics

Note that increases in rent are 'capitalized in the present value of the asset' (see the Business Finance chapter for definition of NPV or net present value), that is properties are partly valued on the basis of the rent they can command.

Conclusion

Once again S & D curves prove useful in illustrating the behaviour of capital markets. Markets for property, of course, behave in much the same way. To a lesser extent 'human markets' of various types of workers can also be represented by S & D curves or, at the very least, demand and supply arguments apply.

ME9. Economic growth and resource conservation

In our discussions of economics much has been said about economic growth (in GNP etc.) and the views on economic control of the Keynesians and monetarists, both camps holding particular views on how growth should be managed. In the long term, however, it has to be born in mind that we have only finite resources and that, partially in response to such constraints, population should stabilize around 2020+. These issues are briefly discussed in the following section.

Market for natural resources

Figure ME24 shows the S & D curves for the market for a natural resource which is common property. For such a resource we define a *reservation price* which is the price of obtaining the resource plus an amount sufficient to compensate for reduction of the resource in future.

Allowing for the reservation price the realistic supply curve is S* and operation moves to E*. Hence operating at point E entailed an efficiency loss equal to the area E*EX.

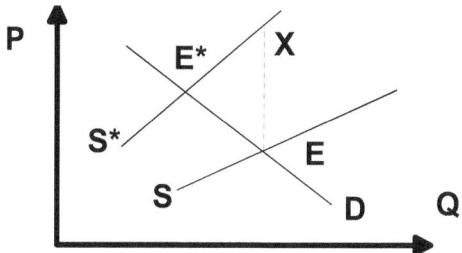

Fig. ME24. Market for natural resource which is common property

Whether the additional funds obtained by using the reservation price could have been obtained by other means, for example, by a special tax, does not alter the basic argument here, namely that it is inefficient (in the long run) not to make such allowance for depletion.

Renewable resources

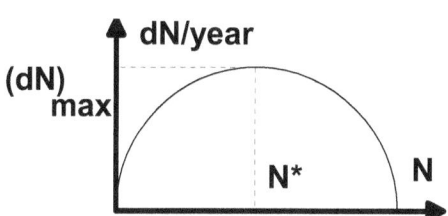

Fig. ME25. Sustainable yield curve.

Figure ME25 shows the sustainable yield curve for a renewable resource, for example a fish population N. For this the curve for the increase per year in this population (dN) is shown, having a maximum $(dN)_{max}$ when $N = N^*$.

The maximum value of dN is the *maximum sustainable yield* and operation at this point will maintain the resource in constant quantity.

3. Microeconomics

When harvesting is depleting such a resource, however, it is important to determine N^* and $(dN)_{max}$ and take appropriate action (such as harvesting at less than $(dN)_{max}$ until the population is restored to N^*).

Non-renewable resources

In the case of non-renewable resources such as oil it is important to have a long term policy. Actions that can be taken in such instances include:

1. Encourage consumption of alternative resources.
2. Produce alternative resources.
3. Develop alternative resources (through R & D, exploration etc.).
4. Encourage responsible usage of limited resources.

Further, as depletion increases the cost of limited resources such changes in consumer behaviour will be encouraged by price pressure.

Overall, or course, it is necessary to control the global population as soon as possible. The majority of this, of course, is not likely to own a car (certainly not a petrol driven one at least), but increasingly depletion of many other resources will be of concern.

Finally, a fine example of the success of policy (3) was the development of synthetic lubricating oils. In the future we might be able to rely on electric cars but they will still need lubricants!

Economic goals

Generally the 'complete overview' figure used for an economy is economic growth (in GNP) and figures often suggested for this were 4%. Lesser figures are appropriate in some economies now, and much larger ones in others.

In fully developed economies the future standard of living is guaranteed by technology (given population stabilizes) and growth economically is not needed in the long term. Indeed in some cases the point has already been reached at which it is necessary to limit growth.

Conclusion

Proper planning is, or course, vital in dealing with limited but renewable resources and with nonrenewable resources. In the latter instance much in the way of alternative product use and development needs to be done. In addition economic growth should be limited in developed economies and population growth must be curtailed globally.

ME10. Income distribution

If we are to have a capitalist or at least free market society then it is necessary to address the question of income distribution or inequality. Clearly there must be, at least apparently, such inequality and the following section discuses this and related issues briefly.

Human Capital

Human capital (investment in education etc.) is the basis of any sensible argument about income distribution, along with net present value (NPV) of income in different occupations.

As an example, suppose we compare the income potential of Mr A and Mr B assuming a discount rate of 10%:

1. A studies to be a surgeon to age 30, then has income $100k til age 55.

2. B becomes a plumber at 20, then has income $20k, increasing at the discount rate to a little over $50k until age 30 and then stabilizing at $50k till age 55.

Comparing their total incomes over time we obtain:

NPV for A at age 30 = $100/(1.1 - 1) = 1000$ ($k)
NPV for B at age 30 = $20(1.1^{10} - 1)/(1.1 - 1) + 50/(1.1 - 1)$
= 819 ($k)

so that B is not so badly off at all. Indeed if he invested some of his earnings when young and relatively uncommitted he could well be ahead.

Hence it is difficult, to say the least, to compare rates of remuneration but equally certain that they cannot be equal at any particular point in time. The long term view must be taken and, moreover, there must be some incentive for those who commit to long studies etc.

Distribution of income

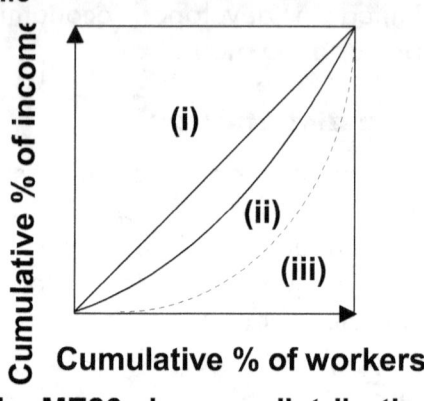

Fig. ME26. Income distribution

Figure ME26 shows typical income distribution curves and the complete equality line:
(i) = complete equality line
(ii) = after tax and transfers
(iii) = actual (Lorentz curve)

It demonstrates that tax and transfer payments (pensions etc.) reduce income equality significantly.

Note, however, that *equality* and *equity* are not synonymous and that equity means 'fair' and that this would should not the basis of income policy. Some occupations requiring exceptional skill and effort, for example, should be remunerated at a higher level than others. Just how high is the real question.

Equal opportunity laws

Equally opportunity, affirmative action and other legislation of similar intent is now commonplace. This is generally intended to give equal access to employment and equal pay where appropriate, but it is not intended to ensure equal pay in general, only to give an 'fair race' so far as competition for remuneration goes.

3. Microeconomics

Poverty

Poverty is unavoidable in any society. Thus to deal with poverty the following things are needed:
1. It is important to define a poverty line to help address the problem more effectively by knowing its magnitude. For this purpose the *Engels coefficient*, that is the proportion of low incomes that is spent on food, is useful (and it takes values of from 0.25 for single persons to 0.33 for small families).
2. Adequate social security arrangements, including child allowances.
3. An infrastructure of emergency and other aid organizations.
4. Training courses for all in need.
5. Subsidized housing.
6. Means of dealing with the welfare trap.

The poverty problem, of course, is much dependent upon unemployment and this has been discussed at a number of points in the text.

Negative income tax?

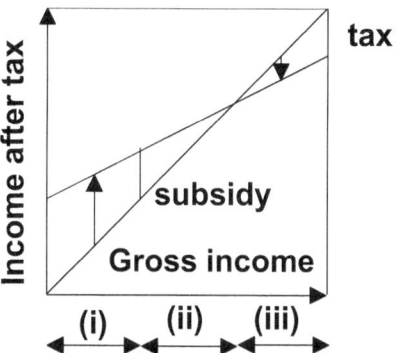

Fig. ME27. Effect of a negative income tax.

Figure ME27 shows the effect of what may seem a novel idea, that is, a negative income tax. With this in region (i) the poor are given a minimum income and this subsidy is tapered and given to all incomes in region (ii). Finally tax proper occurs in region (iii).

3. MICROECONOMICS

In fact this is much the same as the system in place in several countries but the version suggested here might lead to much more drastic leveling of incomes.

The rich

In many counties much effort has been directed at closing tax loopholes and preventing improper business practices. Factors such as company tax rates have to be considered carefully as excessive rates would discourage business expansion and development and hence job creation.

Conclusion

The question of income distribution is a vexatious one. As the example of Mr A and Mr B shows, just what is equitable is not easy to determine. The poverty question too is vexatious, along with that of unemployment. With proper planning, however, much can be done to alleviate these problems.

ME11. Cost functions

In the following section the determination of actual cost functions such as supply and demand curves is discussed. Then examples of such functions are given and the simple mathematical manipulations required to use them are demonstrated.

Determination of cost functions

To determine the data for a function $y = f(x)$ of a production process cost (y) where x is the number of units produced the following guidelines are useful:

1. x and y must be related (by such a function).
2. Production should be observed when production is 'constant' or steady.
3. Sufficient observations must be made to give a reasonable spread of data (in fact the range of production is often underestimated).
4. Observations of variations in y as a result only of those in x are required (and not as a result of other contributing factors).

Then a suspected form for the function must be established. Usually a polynomial function with unknown coefficients is used and the values of the coefficients can be determined by linear regression (see Section IE11).

Short and long run supply curves

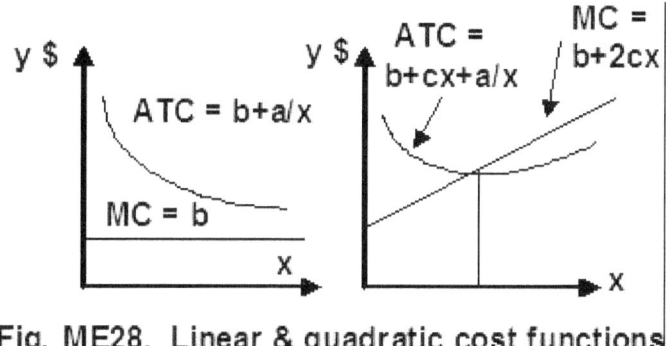

Fig. ME28. Linear & quadratic cost functions

Suppose the long run supply curve for a production process has been found to be of the form

(ME3) $y = a + bx - cx^2 + dx^3$

where a minus sign for c is often the suspected form for such curves.

Then the average total cost (ATC) and marginal cost (MC) are immediately given as

(ME4) $y/x = ATC = a/x + b - cx + dx^2$

(ME5) $dy/dx = MC = b - 2cx + 3dx^2$

In practice, in fact, linear and quadratic cost functions are generally satisfactory and examples of these are shown in Figure ME28.

3. MICROECONOMICS

Finally, for the minimum in ATC shown in Figure ME28(b), we have the *marginal average cost* given by the quotient rule of differentiation:

(ME6) $\qquad d(y/x)/dx = (xy' - y)/x^2$

(ME7) $\qquad\qquad\qquad = 0$ when $y' = y/x$

so that the minimum in the ATC curve occurs when marginal cost (MC) equals average cost (ATC), that is the MC curve intersects the average (total) cost curve at its minimum point, as assumed in Section ME2. As pointed out there, this is the break-even point for production.

Demand functions

As an example assume that demand x and price S are related by

(ME8) $\qquad 2x + S^2 - 12000 = 0$

giving

(ME9) $\quad p(x) = \sqrt{(12000 - 2x)}$

as the demand function and this is shown in Figure ME29.

Fig. ME29. Quadratic demand function

Then it follows immediately that
(ME10) $\qquad$ marginal demand function = $p'(x)$
(ME11) $\qquad$ (total) revenue function = $R(x) = xp(x)$
(ME12) $\qquad$ marginal revenue function = $R'(x)$
$\qquad\qquad\qquad = (12000 - 3x)/\sqrt{(12000 - 2x)}$

and setting the latter to zero gives $x = 4000$ as the number of units produced for maximum revenue, each at price $p(x) = \$ 63.25$, so that the maximum revenue is $R(x = 4000) = 4000(63.25) = \$ 235,000$.

3. Microeconomics

Profit functions

Profit functions are given by subtracting the production cost function $y = C(x)$ from the revenue function $R(x)$:

(ME13) $P(x) = R(x) - C(x)$

and the marginal profit function is given by

(ME14) $P'(x) = R'(x) - C'(x)$

so that profit is maximum when

(ME15) $R'(x) = C'(x)$

so that maximum profit occurs when marginal revenue and marginal cost are equal and, it then follows from Equation ME7, these are both then equal to the average cost y/x.

As an example let $C(x) = x^3 - 3x^2 - 80x + 500$ and $S = 2800$ so that $R(x) = 2800x$. Then equating $C'(x)$ and $R'(x)$ we obtain

(ME16) $3x^2 - 6x - 80 = 2800$ or $x^2 - 2x - 960 = 0$

Factorizing this gives $(x - 32)(x + 30) = 0$
giving the roots $x = 32$ and $x = -30$.

Then with the 'sensible' solution $x = 32$ we test the nature of the turning point:

(ME17) $p''(x) = R''(x) - C''(x) = 0 - (6x - 6) = -6(32) + 6 < 0$

so that the turning point is a maximum and the value of the profit at this maximum is given by

$P(32) = 2800(32) - [32^3 - 3(32)^2) - 80(32) + 500] = \$ 61,964$

Conclusion

Once they have been determined (for example by regression) cost functions are easy to use to determine intersection points and maxima, such points having the applications described in preceding sections of this and the preceding chapter.

3. MICROECONOMICS

References

Batra R, *Surviving the Great Depression of 1990*, Bantam/Schwartz, Sydney/Melbourne 1989.

Bowman, RG, Buchanan J, The efficient market hypothesis - a discussion of institutional, agency and behavioural issues, *Australian J. Management*, vol. 20, n2, 1995.

Cipolla CM, *The Economic History of World Population*, 6th edn, Penguin, Harmondsworth 1974.

Cole CL, *Microeconomics: A Contemporary Approach*, Harcourt Brace Jovanovich, New York 1973.

Cole CL, Baumol WJ, *Microeconomics: A Contemporary Approach,* Harcourt Brace Jovanovich, New York 1973.

Davies JR, Hughes S, *Managerial Economics*, MacDonald & Evans, Plymouth 1977.

Elkan W., *An Introduction to Developmental Economics*, Penguin, Harmonsworth 1973.

Galbraith, JK, *The Liberal Hour*, Pelican, Harmondsworth, 1963.

Gibson G, Hermann A, Kirkwood L, Swiericzuk J, *The Australian Economy: An Overview*, Pitman, Melbourne, 1977. *Problems and Issues*, Pitman, Melbourne, 1978. *Management and Policies*, Pitman, Melbourne 1979.

Hicks JR, *The Social Framework*, 3rd edn, OUP, Oxford 1960.

Meadows DH, Meadows DL, Randers J, Behrens WW, *The Limits to Growth, Pan*, London. 1972.

Hocking A (ed.), *Investigating Economics*, 2nd edn, Longman Cheshire, Melbourne 1980.

Mohr GA, Numerical procedures for input-output analysis, Applied Mathematics & Computation, vol. 101, pp 89-98, 1999.

Mohr G.A., *Elementary Thinking for the 21st Century*, Xlibris, Sydney, 2014.

Mohr GA, *The Scientific MBA,* 5th edn, Balboa Press, Bloomington, Indiana, 2017.

Mohr GA, *Elementary Thinking for Modern Management,* Amazon-Kindle, 2018.

Nankervis FT, Descriptive Economics: *The Australian Economic Structure, 2nd edn*, Longman, Green & Co., Melbourne 1956.

Packard V, *The Waste Makers*, Pelican, Harmondsworth 1963.

Pearce DW, Turner RK, *Economics of Natural Resources and the Environment*, Harvester Wheatsheaf, Hemel Hempstead 1990.

Quayle M, Robinso T, McEachem W, Microeconomics: A Contemporary Introduction, Nelson, Melbourne 1994.

Noble CE, *Australian Economic Terms,* 2nd edn, Longman Cheshire, Melbourne 1980.

Sweezy PM, *The Theory of Capitalist Development*, Dennis Dobson Ltd, London 1946.

Reineck I, *The Money Masters: Banks, Power and Economic Control*, Heinemann, Melbourne 1988.

Waud, RN, *Microeconomics*, 3rd edn, Harper & Row, New York, NY 1986.

Williams M, Stevenson K, *Australia, A Mixed Economy*, Longman Cheshire, Melbourne 1981.

Wonnacott P, Wonnacott R, *Economics*, McGraw-Hill, New York 1979.

3. Microeconomics

Chapter 4

TIME STEPPING ECONOMIC MODELS

> *If all economists were laid end to end,*
> *they would not reach a conclusion.*
> George Bernard Shaw (attributed to).

Time stepping of economic models

Klein modeled the performance of the US economy in the years 1921 - 1941 using three *structural equations* (in $B US):

(4.1) $C = 16.8 + 0.02P + 0.23P_L + 0.8(W + S)$

(4.2) $I = 17.8 + 0.23P + 0.55P_L - 0.15K_L$

(4.3) $W = 1.6 + 0.42X + 0.16X_L + 0.131t - |1931|$

where $|t - 1931|$ is a heavy side step function (i.e., = 0 of $t <$ 1931 and = 1 if $t > 1931$) and subscript 'L' denotes 'last value/year', and adding three *definitive equations*:

(4.4) $X = C + I + G$

(4.5) $P = X - W - T$

(4.6) $K = K_L + I$

where C = total consumption, I = total investment, W, S are the private/public sector wages, X is the private sector production, P is the profits (nonwage income), K = stocks (capital goods at end of year), G = government spending, T = business taxes and subscript L denotes value for the previous year. In the above, t, S, G, T are exogenous, that is, a set of independent variables.

4. TIME STEPPING ECONOMIC MODELS

We can make the model more 'self contained' by assuming tax rate $t = 0.2$ so that

(4.7) $\qquad S = (1 - t) G = 0.8G$ and $T = t(W_L + P_L)$

and including these in Klein's equations.

Then the equations can be rearranged and written in the matrix form

$$A\{V\} = \begin{bmatrix} 1 & 0 & -0.8 & 0 & -0.02 & 0 \\ 0 & 1 & 0 & 0 & -0.23 & 0 \\ 0 & 0 & 1 & -0.42 & 0 & 0 \\ -1 & -1 & 0 & 1 & 0 & 0 \\ 0 & 0 & 1.0 & -1 & 1.0 & 0 \\ 0 & -1 & 0 & 0 & 0 & 1 \end{bmatrix} \begin{Bmatrix} C \\ I \\ W \\ X \\ P \\ K \end{Bmatrix} = \begin{Bmatrix} Q_1 \\ Q_2 \\ Q_3 \\ G \\ 0 \\ K_L \end{Bmatrix}$$

where $Q_1 = 16.8 + 0.23 P_L + 0.8 S$ (and $S = 0.8 G$)

$Q_2 = 17.8 + 0.55 P_L - 0.15 K_L$

$Q_3 = 1.6 + 0.16 X_L + 0.131 t - t_0 I$

Now they can be coded and 'time stepping method' and Gauss Jordan reduction (for matrix inversion) used to solve for the variables $\{V\}$ after each of a succession of one year steps.

This is done in the following Visual Basic program:

```
Public output As Object
Sub main()
Set output = Form1
output.Line (0, 0)-(0, 0): output.DrawWidth = 5
output.Font.Size = 16
output.Font.Bold = Not output.Font.Bold
5 Dim A(6, 6), Q(6), R(6), V(6), S(6), F(6), PR(100, 2), FR(6), L(6), C$(6)
10 For J = 1 To 6: S(J) = 0: F(J) = 1.4: L(J) = 0: Next J
12 C$(1) = "C": C$(2) = "I": C$(3) = "W": C$(4) = "X": C$(5) = "P": C$(6) = "K"
15 F(6) = 2: Rem S(2)=100:S(3)=100:S(5)=100
20 N = 6: z = 0:: D = 0: K1 = 100: X1 = 100: P1 = 10: W1 = 25
```

4. Time Stepping Economic Models

```
25 For I = 1 To N: For J = 1 To N: A(I, J) = 0: Next J: A(I, I) = 1: Next I
26 A(1, 3) = -0.8: A(1, 5) = -0.02: A(2, 5) = -0.23: A(3, 4) = -0.42
27 A(4, 1) = -1: A(4, 2) = -1: A(5, 3) = 1: A(5, 4) = -1: A(6, 2) = -1
29 GoTo 100
30 T = 0.4: G = 0.8: D = 0: z = z + 1: If z > 30 Then GoTo 85
31 Rem If z > 10 And z < 21 Then D = z - 10
32 If z = 10 Or z = 11 Then T = 0.4: G = 1
33 Rem ? "IP - if 99 then end":input g,t:if g=99 goto 85
35 R(2) = 17.8 + 0.55 * P1 - 0.15 * K1: R(3) = 1.6 + 0.16 * X1 + 0.13 * D: R(6) = K1
40 R(5) = -T * (W1 + P1): R(4) = -G * R(5)
42 SV = 0.2 * R(4): R(1) = 16.8 + 0.23 * P1 + 0.8 * SV
45 For I = 1 To N: Q(I) = 0: For K = 1 To N
50 Q(I) = Q(I) + A(I, K) * R(K): Next K: Next I
55 For J = 1 To N: V(J) = (2 * Q(J) + S(J)) / F(J)
60 XI = 300 * (z - 2): YI = 6000 - 30 * L(J)
65 X = 300 * (z - 1): Y = 6000 - 30 * V(J): output.Line (XI, YI)-(X, Y)
66 P = 10 * Int(Y / 10) + 2: If z < 30 Then GoTo 68
67 output.PSet (9000, P): output.Print C$(J)
output.PSet (1000, 500): output.Print Q(4), Q(5)
68 Next J
69 Debug.Print z, "AP =", Q(4), "P =", Q(5), D
70 P1 = Q(5): X1 = Q(4): K1 = Q(6): W1 = Q(3)
75 For J = 1 To N: L(J) = V(J): Next J
80 PR(z, 1) = P1: PR(z, 2) = K1
82 GoTo 30
85 For I = 1 To N: FR(I) = Q(I): Next I
86 output.Line (0, 0)-(0, 7000): output.Line (0, 6000)-(9000, 6000)
90 GoTo 130
100 For I = 1 To N: X = A(I, I): A(I, I) = 1
105 For J = 1 To N: A(I, J) = A(I, J) / X: Next J
110 For K = 1 To N: If K = I Then GoTo 120
112 X = A(K, I): A(K, I) = 0
115 For J = 1 To N: A(K, J) = A(K, J) - X * A(I, J): Next J
120 Next K: Next I
125 GoTo 30
130 Printer.EndDoc
135 End Sub
```

Here the initial values of *P* etc. are set in line 20 and the values chosen in Equations 4.7 are set in line 30.

4. Time Stepping Economic Models

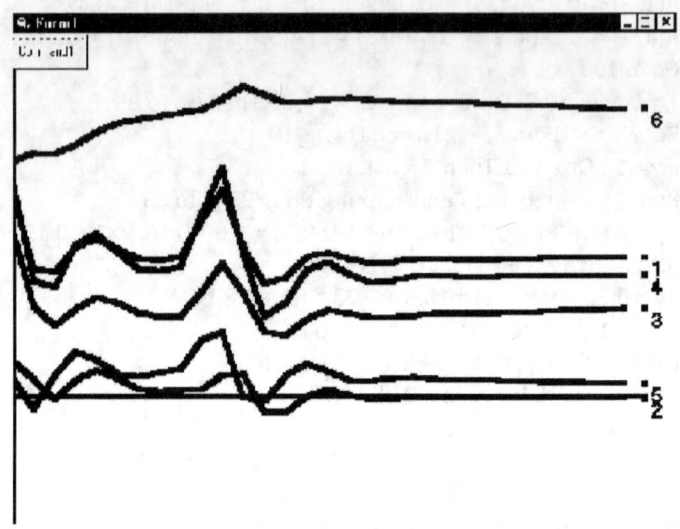

Figure 4.1. Output from time stepping program.

Figure 4.1 shows the results with changes in *T* and *G* only occurring at years 10 and 11 (set in line 32 of the program), giving the expected disturbance in activity.

Alternatively, D = D + 1 can be set after the tenth iteration/year (z in the program) to activate Klein's original step function 'after 1931 term' in Equation 4.3.

References

Hunt, E.K. and Sherman, H.J. *Economics: An Introduction to Traditional and Radical Views*, 4th edn. Harper & Row, New York, 1981.

L.R. Klein, *Economic Fluctuations in the United States, 1921-1941*, John Wiley & Sons, New York, 1950.

Mohr, G.A. Time Stepping of Macroeconomic Models, *Applied Mathematics & Computation*, Vol. 102, pp 273-278, 1999.

Chapter 5

THE LMS AND ISE CURVES

> *A third feature of this book is that it introduces both consumption and investment expenditures as sensitive to the interest rate in the initial IS-LM model presentation. Treating consumption expenditures as sensitive to the interest rate in the analytical chapters is important because the modern theoretical and empirical view is that such a relationship exists.*
> Jack Vernon, *Macroeconomics* (1980).

A concise but complete macroeconomic model

The following is a very brief summary of the book by Vernon quoted from above. Herein the basic GNP equations (in simple form) are developed into a fairly complete model which can be used to estimate magnitudes of actions required attain objectives such as full employment.

Extending Vernon's equations for the LMS (liquid money supply) and ISE (interest sensitive expenditure) curves somewhat, it is shown that *increasing interest rates increases inflation,* as intuition suggests, and contrary to current economic practice by central banks.

1. FISCAL MODEL

Equilibrium:
Aggregate supply/output Q = E
the aggregate real demand/expenditure
$= C + I$ or consumption + investment
$= a + bQ^* + I = 50 + 0.8Q^* + 70$ \hfill (5.1)

5. THE LMS AND ISE CURVES

where Q^* = real private disposable income = Q assumed here
and $\delta C/\delta Q^* = b$ = marginal propensity to consume (MPC)
giving
$$Q = (a + I)/(1 - b) = (50 + 70)/0.2 = 600$$
with $1/(1 - b)$ = consumption multiplier

Full employment constraint:
$$Q_f = 1000 = \text{full employment output}$$

Consider three cases:

(a) With $I = 70$ (as above) Equation (1) gives
$$E = 50 + 0.8(1000) + 70 = 920$$
   - this is greater than the equilibrium demand (600) so we have shortfall (in production) unemployment.

(b) $I = 150$ gives $Q = (a + I)/(1 - b) = (50 + 150)/(1 - 0.8) = 1000$
giving: full employment
$$E = 50 + 0.8(1000) + 150 = 1000$$
so that we have equilibrium and thus constant prices (or zero inflation)

(c) $I = 230$ gives $E = 50 + 0.8(1000) + 230 = 1080$
giving an expenditure gap = $E - Q_f = 80$ with demand > supply and prices rise

Note: (1) MPC reduces with income level: e.g.

Income (after tax)	Consumption	MPC
3,000	5,000	1.67
30,000	24,000	0.80

and MPC also tends to decrease with time (i.e. we 'get wise')

(2) Time series analysis gives results for the regression line such as:
$$C = 1.51 \, (\$B) + 0.91 Q^* \quad \text{with b in the range 0.88 to 0.92}$$

5. The LMS and ISE curves

Government purchases:

$$E = C + I + G \quad \text{with } C = a + b(Q - T + D) \tag{5.2}$$

$a = 50$, $I = 70$ still and let $G = 80$

T = real Gov. tax receipts = 200

D = real Gov. transfer payments = 100

giving $C = 50 + 0.8Q + 0.8(-200 + 100) = -30 + 0.8Q$

so that we have $\quad E = C + I + G = 120 + 0.8Q \tag{5.3}$

Considering the same three cases:

(a) $Q = E$ (equilibrium ignoring the full employment constraint)

gives $Q = 120/0.2 = 600$

and shortfall unemployment with

$C = -30 + 0.8(600) = 450$, $I = 70$, $G = 80$

(b) using *discretionary fiscal ease* to obtain full employment we:

(i) use $\delta G = 80$ giving from Equation (3)

$$E = 200 + 0.8(Q_f = 1000) = 1000$$

and $Q = (a - bT + bD + I + G)/(1 - b)$ from Equation (2)

with $E = Q = (50 - 160 + 80 + 70 + 160)/0.2 = 1000$

(ii) or $\delta T = -5$ or $dD = 5$ gives $dE = 4$

so that we need change in T or D of magnitude 100 for full employment.

(c) using *discretionary fiscal restraint* we do the reverse of (b), that is we have $\delta G = -80$

or $\quad \delta T = 100$ or $\delta D = -100$

which when $I = 230$ so that $E = 50 + 0.8(1000) + 230 = 1080$ gives the required change (in the original case (c) above).

5. THE LMS AND ISE CURVES

Including tax rate:
$$Q = E \text{ (for equilibrium)} = a + b[(1 - t)Q - T + D] + I + G$$

where disposable income Q^* (assumed $= Q$) is reduced by tax rate t, and now T is a tax constant,

giving $\delta Q/\delta I = 1/[1 - b(1 - t)] = 2.5$ (not 5 as before) with $t = 0.25$

and $\delta Q/\delta T = -b/[1 - b(1 - t)] = -2$ (not -4 as before)

$\delta Q/\delta D = b/[1 - b(1 - t)] = 2$ (not 4 as before)

and these multipliers are reduced further when monetary policy is included.

2. MONETARY MODEL

Money supply MS = MD the money demand (both real)

where MS = M/P with P = price level factor = 1 assumed

$$MD = f(Q, r); \quad I = f(r); \quad C = f(Q^*, r) \quad (r = \text{interest rate})$$

For demand we have $E = C + I^* + G$

with C = consumption expenditure function $= a + bQ^* - sr$

where s = interest responsiveness of C
$= 50 + 0.8Q^* - 1000r$ with $Q^* = Q(1 - t) - T + D = Q - 50 + 75$

where T = tax constant and t = tax rate
I = investment expenditure function $= I^* - ir$
where i = interest responsiveness of I
(early versions of the Fed-MIT model take s approx. = i)

$= 200 - 1000r$
and $G = 230$
so that $E = E^* + b(1 - t)Q - (i + s)r$

with $E^* = a - bT + bD + I + G$
$= 50 - 40 + 60 + 200 + 230 = 500$
so that $E = Q$ for equilibrium gives

$r = \{E^* - [1 - b(1- t)]Q\}/(i + s) = (500 - 0.4Q)/2000 = 0.25 - 0.0002Q$
(5.4)

and this is the *interest sensitive expenditure (ISE) curve* - a 'down' demand curve with r the up/price axis and Q the cross/quantity axis.

5. THE LMS AND ISE CURVES

For supply MS = M/P = 200/P = 200
$$= MD = L + kQ - qr$$

with L = money demand constant = 50
k = income responsiveness of money demand = 0.2
and q = interest responsiveness of money demand = 1000
giving:
$$r = (L - M/P + kQ)/q = -0.15 + 0.0002Q \qquad (5.5)$$

and this is the *liquid money supply curve* (LMS curve) - an 'up' supply curve

and summing the two equations 5.4 and 5.5 gives 2r = 0.10 or r = 0.05 whence Q = 1000.

Then $\delta C/\delta r = -s = -1000$ and $\delta I/\delta r = -i = -1000$

so that an increase of 1% in r gives decrease of 10 $B in both C and I*.

Note: we have here kQ = M/P (if r = 0, L = 0) or M(V = 1/k) = PQ if we compare with the classical velocity of money theory, whence velocity = 1/k

Then if we have $\delta I = 80$ so that I = 280 (giving an expenditure gap = 80) this gives the ISE curve r = 0.29 - 0.0002Q

and if P = 1.25 the LMS curve is r = -0.11 + 0.0002Q

Solving the two equations (by summing them to give 2r = 0.18) gives
$$r = 0.09 \text{ and } Q = 0.2/0.0002 = 1000$$

as the point of intersection (and equilibrium) and the gap is removed.

Aggregate savings approach:

Define aggregate saving = S = Q - (C + G)   (= I at equilibrium)
= SP + SG where SP = private = Q* - C = Q - T + D - C
SG = government = T + tQ - D - G
giving S = Q - {a + b[(1 - t)Q - T + D] - sr} - G
= - a + bT - bD - G + [1 - b(1 - t)]Q + sr
= - 50 + 40 - 60 - 230 + 0.4Q + 1000r
= - 300 + 0.4Q + 1000r

5. THE LMS AND ISE CURVES

and SP = Q - T + D -{a + b[(1 - t)Q -T + D] - sr}
     = Q - 50 + 75 - {50 + 0.6Q - 40 + 60 - 1000r}
     = - 45 + 0.15Q + 1000r
   SG = T + tQ - D - G = 50 + 0.25Q - 75 - 230 = - 255 + 0.25Q

and these sum to give S as required.

Then I = 200 - 1000r (from previously)
        = -300 + 0.4Q + 1000r

giving r = 0.25 - 0.0002Q or the original ISE curve of Equation (5.4) with r = .05 and Q = 1000 at the equilibrium point and S = 150 = I; SP = 155, so that SG = -5 (in deficit).

Interest rates and inflation

Most economists still mistakenly believe that increasing interest rates reduces inflation. They argue that as interest rates are reduced, people are able to borrow more money, so that consumers have more money to spend, causing the economy to grow and inflation to increase.

Intuition suggests otherwise because greater interest rates increase company debt repayments, leading to higher costs which are passed on to the consumer and the economy at large.

The proof is found using the equations of the *liquid money supply* (LMS) and *interest sensitive expenditure* (ISE) curves.

With the minor modification transfer payments $D = f(r)$, the proof is as follows:

Real money supply = MS = M/P
                 = money demand = MD = L + kQ - qr

where P = price inflation = 1
M is non-inflation deflated money supply = 200
L is money demand constant = 50
Q is total output
r is the official interest rate
k is income responsiveness of money demand = 0.2
q is interest responsiveness of money demand = 1,000

5. THE LMS AND ISE CURVES

giving for the LMS curve:

$$qr - kQ = L - M/P \qquad (5.6)$$

For demand, we have expenditure $E = C + I + G$

with C the consumption expenditure function $= a + bQ^* - sr$
where $a = 50$, $b = 0.8$, $s =$ interest responsiveness of $C = 1,000$
so that $C = 50 + 0.8Q^* - 1,000r$
with $Q^* = Q(1 - t) - T + D$
where T is the tax constant, t is the tax rate,
D is the transfer payments,
and I is the investment expenditure function:

$$= I^* - ir = 200 - 1,000r$$

where i is interest responsiveness of I and $i = 1,000$
(early versions of the Fed-MIT model take s approx. $= i$)
and G is equal to 230 (government spending)

so that $E = E^* + b(1 - t)Q - (i + s)r$

with $E^* = a - bT + bD + I^* + G$

where $a = 50$, $b = 0.8$, $t = 0.25$, $T = 50$, $I^* = 200$, $G = 230$

Now let $D =$ transfer payments $= D^* + yU$
with $D^* = 25$, $y = 1,000$
where $U =$ unemployment rate $= U^* + r/2$ with $U^* = 0.025$

so that $E^* = a - bT + bD^* + byU^* + byr/2 + I^* + G$

Then $E = Q$ for equilibrium gives

$$Q = a - bT + bD^* + byU^* + byr/2 + I^* + G + b(1 - t)Q - (i + s)r$$

or

$$(i + s - by/2)r + [1 - b(1 - t)]Q = a - bT + bD^* + byU^* + I^* + G \qquad (5.7)$$

and this is the ISE curve, a 'down' demand curve.

Solving Equations (5.6) and (5.7) gives the equilibrium values of r and Q (and thence U).
With the values of constants stated above, we obtain

$$1,000r - 0.2Q = -150 \qquad (5.8a)$$

$$1,600r + 0.4Q = 480 \qquad (5.8b)$$

5. THE LMS AND ISE CURVES

Adding twice the first to the second gives $r = 0.05$ and thence $Q = 1,000$ and $U = 0.05$.

With inflation $P = 1.1$, however, the solution is

$r = 0.0601,$ $Q = 959.6,$ and $U = 0.0551.$

Looking in reverse, this shows that increasing interest rates to 6% will cause 10% inflation, increase unemployment by 0.5%, and reduce total output by 4%.

To prove this beyond doubt, put $r = 0.0601$ in Equation 5.8b [not Equation 5.8a as this originally involved P which is now taken unknown], giving $Q = 959.6$ and put these values of r and Q (and $L = 50$, $M = 200$, $q = 1,000$, $k = 0.2$) in Equation 5.6, giving $P = 1.10$.

The bottom line is that increasing official interest rates increases inflation, as intuition would suggest.

Indeed, in Australia's economic history of the last 60 years, there has only been one instance of interest rates and inflation going in opposite directions, this being some time after the OPEC oil shocks of 1979/80 and the floating of the Australian dollar in 1983.

In the USA it has been a similar story.

Figure 5.1 charts the US federal funds rate and the rate of inflation from 1954 to 2019, 1954 being the first year in which the US government set the 'official cash rate', as it is called in Australia.

Here the generally higher plot (with dashed lines) is the funds rate, the lower (with solid lines) being the inflation rate.

The chart clearly shows a general trend for the inflation rate to increase when the funds rate increases, and to decrease when the funds rate decreases.

The extreme 18% interest rate in 1980 was in response to a recession, whilst the zero interest rate from 2008 to 2014 was in response to the 2008 'financial crisis', the very opposite nature of these responses being puzzling, to say the least.

5. THE LMS AND ISE CURVES

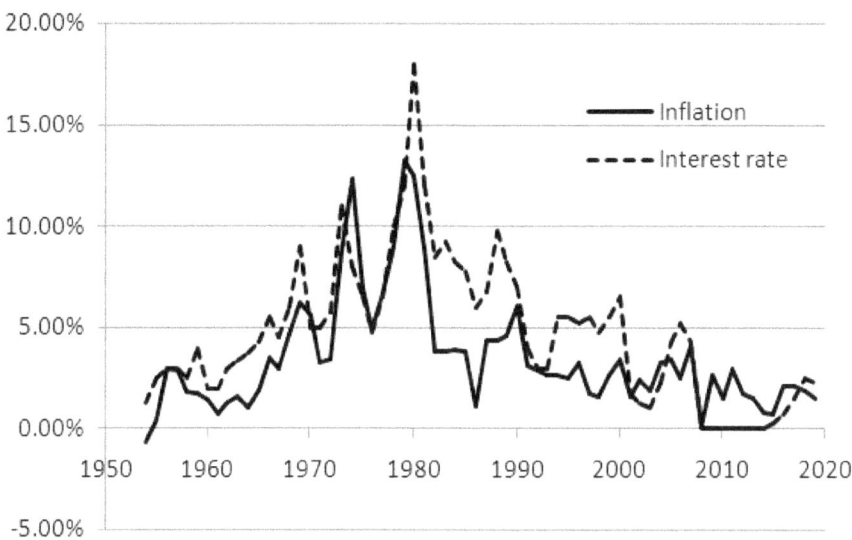

Figure 5.1. The US federal funds rate (the generally higher plot) and inflation from 1954 to 2019.

The author was in New Zealand in the early 1980s, and well recalls New Zealand's official interest rate rising to circa 18% by 1984, no doubt influenced by the US rate. He quit his University job and sold his part-owned house and returned to Australia at the end of that year, losing a good deal of money because Australia's official interest rate was much lower than the New Zealand one at the time.

No doubt some local 'money traders' made a lot of money out of that difference in official interest rates at the time!

References

Benham, F. *Economics*, 6th edn., Pitman, London, 1960.

Caves RE, Frankel JA, Jones RW, *World Trade and Payments: An Introduction,* Scott Foresman/Little Brown, Glenview IL (1990).

5. THE LMS AND ISE CURVES

Hunt, E.K. and Sherman, H.J. *Economics: An Introduction to Traditional and Radical Views,* 4th edn, Harper & Row, New York. 1981.

Mohr GA, *The Pretentious Persuaders,* Horizon, Sydney (2012, 2014 – 2nd edition).

Mohr GA, *The Doomsday Calculation,* Xlibris, Sydney (2012b).

Mohr GA, *Elementary Thinking for the 21st Century,* Xlibris, Sydney (2014).

Mohr GA, Fear E, *The Brainwashed: From Consumer Zombies to Islamism and Jihad,* Inspiring Publishers, Canberra (2016).

Mohr GA, *The Scientific MBA,* 5th ed., Balboa Press, Bloomington IN (2017).

Mohr GA, *Elementary Thinking for Modern Management,* Amazon-Kindle (2018).

Mohr GA, Mohr PE, Mohr RS, *Brainwashed Zombies: Religious, Political & Consumer Persuasion,* Amazon-Kindle (2018).

Vernon, Jack, *Macroeconomics* (2nd end), The Dryden Press, Hinsdale IL (1980).

Tarshis, L. *Modern Economics.* Houghton Mifflin, Boston. 1967.

Vernon, J. *Macroeconomics.* The Dryden Press, Hinsdale IL, 1980.

Wells, S.J. *International Economics,* Allen & Unwin, London, 1969.

Wonnacott, P. and Wonnacott, R. *Economics,* McGraw-Hill, New York, 1979.

Chapter 6

INPUT-OUTPUT ANALYSIS

> *Input-output analysis is one of the most important tools of management science, one ideally suited for today's ubiquitous PC.* G. A. Mohr, in a 1999 paper on IOA.

Input-Output Analysis

This important technique was developed by Wassily Leontief at Harvard in 1931 and his study of the US economy with it gained a Nobel Prize. Later, Laurence Klein applied IOA to the world economy, also receiving a Nobel Prize.

As a simple example of IOA consider three companies X, Y and Z that sell/buy products/materials to/from each other, the value of these transactions over some regular period being shown in Table 6.1.

Table 6.1. Input-output analysis data

	Purchases				Total
	X	Y	Z	External	Output ($)
Sales					
X	-	60	40	100	200
Y	40	-	100	260	400
Z	50	100	-	50	200
Labour	110	240	60	-	410
Total input	200	400	200	410	1,210

This table also includes labour costs for the period, as well as *external* sales (other than to the other two companies). Then company Y, for example, sells $40 of goods to X and $100 to Z, the remaining $260 of its total output ($400) being sold externally.

6. INPUT-OUTPUT ANALYSIS

To produce this output Y purchases $60 in goods from X and $100 from Z, also spending $240 on labour costs.

Then from Table 6.1 we can easily calculate *input coefficients* by dividing the three X,Y,Z columns by their totals, giving the results shown in Table 6.2.

Table 6.2. Input coefficients

	X	Y	Z
X	-	0.15	0.2
Y	0.2	-	0.5
Z	0.25	0.25	-
Labour	0.55	0.6	0.3

Then for company Y, for example, Table 6.2 shows that for each $1 of output produced 15 cents is spent on purchases from X, 25 cents on purchases from Z and 60 cents is spent on labour costs.

Then using the coefficients of Table 6.2 we can write the outputs x, y, z for companies X, Y, Z as:

$$x = 0.15y + 0.20z + 100 \quad (6.1a)$$

$$y = 0.20x + 0.50z + 260 \quad (6.1b)$$

$$z = 0.25x + 0.25y + 50 \quad (6.1c)$$

Now suppose we wish to determine the effect of increasing the external sales of X to $120 (from $100). Then we change the last number in Equation 6.1a and rearrange the equations to give:

$$\begin{bmatrix} 1 & -0.15 & -0.20 \\ -0.20 & 1 & -0.50 \\ -0.25 & -0.25 & 1 \end{bmatrix} \begin{Bmatrix} x \\ y \\ x \end{Bmatrix} = \begin{Bmatrix} 120 \\ 260 \\ 50 \end{Bmatrix} \quad (6.2)$$

and solving these equations we obtain

$$x = \$223, \quad y = \$408, \quad z = \$208$$

6. INPUT-OUTPUT ANALYSIS

From these results we are then, for example, able to calculate the increased labour costs resulting for each company as:

X: 223 x 0.55 = 122.7   (increase of $12.7)
Y: 408 x 0.60 = 244.8   (increase of $4.8)
Z: 208 x 0.30 = 62.4   (increase of $2.4)

Here a 'flow through' effect to other companies is immediately apparent (a more superficial approach would predict the increase in labour cost for X as increase in external output (20) multiplied by 0.55 = $11 and effects on other companies would be neglected).

Conclusion

Input-output analysis is an important technique and a program (whose inversion routine uses pivoting) for solving IOA problems is given in the following section.

The following QBASIC program solves the foregoing IOA problem using an inversion routine (INVERTA) which includes pivoting, using a *flag vector* M( ) to record column/row swaps and another vector (i.e. column matrix) is used to store columns during swapping.

```
DECLARE SUB inverta (A!(), n!)
  n = 3: DIM M(n, n), X(n), B(n)
  B(1) = 120: B(2) = 260: B(3) = 50
  FOR I = 1 TO n: FOR J = 1 TO n
  READ M(I, J): NEXT: NEXT
  inverta M(), n
  FOR I = 1 TO 3: FOR J = 1 TO 3
  X(I) = X(I) + M(I, J) * B(J): NEXT: NEXT
  PRINT "Solution"
  FOR I = 1 TO 3: PRINT I, " = ", X(I): NEXT: END
  DATA 1,-0.15,-0.2
  DATA -0.2,1,-0.5
  DATA -0.25,-0.25,1
```

6. INPUT-OUTPUT ANALYSIS

```
SUB inverta (A(), n)
REM Inversion routine with pivoting
   DIM M(n), COL(n): AMIN = 1E-20
   FOR I = 1 TO n: M(I) = -I: NEXT
   FOR II = 1 TO n: D = 0
   FOR J = 1 TO n: IF M(J) > 0 THEN 100
   FOR I = 1 TO n: IF M(I) > 0 THEN 90
   IF ABS(D) >= ABS(A(I, J)) THEN 90
   L = J: K = I: D = A(I, J)
90 NEXT I
100 NEXT J
   TEMP = -M(L): M(L) = M(K): M(K) = TEMP
   FOR I = 1 TO n: COL(I) = A(I, L): A(I, L) = A(I, K)
   A(I, K) = COL(I): NEXT I
   IF ABS(D) <= AMIN THEN PRINT "SINGULAR"
   FOR J = 1 TO n: A(K, J) = -A(K, J) / D: NEXT
   FOR I = 1 TO n: IF I = K THEN 180
   FOR J = 1 TO n: A(I, J) = A(I, J) + COL(I) * A(K, J): NEXT J
180 NEXT I
   COL(K) = 1
   FOR I = 1 TO n: A(I, K) = COL(I) / D: NEXT
   NEXT II
   FOR I = 1 TO n: IF M(I) = I THEN 270
   FOR L = 1 TO n: IF M(L) = I THEN 240
   NEXT L
240 M(L) = M(I): M(I) = I
   FOR J = 1 TO n: TEMP = A(L, J): A(L, J) = A(I, J)
   A(I, J) = TEMP: NEXT J
270 NEXT I
END SUB
```

The data used in the listing is that for the IOA problem of Equation 6.2.

6. INPUT-OUTPUT ANALYSIS

Optimizing IOA problems

The foregoing problem can be optimized by choosing the unconstrained objective function

$$f_u = x_1 + x_2 + x_3 \qquad (6.3)$$

subject to the constraints

$$x_i \geq 0 \qquad (6.4)$$

$$(x_i - x_{av}) = 0 \qquad (6.5)$$

which allow only positive x_i and we seek to make them equal (to an average value) and are applied using the penalty augmented objective function

$$f = f_u + \beta \Sigma(x_i - x_{av})^2 + \beta \Sigma x_i^2 \mid x_i < 0 \qquad (6.6)$$

Using the off-diagonal input coefficients as design variables a 'gradient matrix' for minimization by steepest descent is given by

$$[G_{ij}] = [\delta f / \delta M_{ij}] \quad i \neq j \qquad (6.7)$$

where $\delta M_{ij} = M_{ij}/10$ is used as a perturbation.

Then trial searches of length S are conducted with the trial M matrix given by

$$M'_{ij} = M_{ij} - SG_{ij} \quad i \neq j \qquad (6.8)$$

to find a minimum in f, disallowing off diagonal values of M_{ij} greater than -0.05.

With only $\beta = 1$ successive searches are
 $S = 0.0000043, \ f = 8290, \ f_u = 1106$
 $S = 0.0000024, \ f = 7110, \ f_u = 1114$
 $S = 0.0000071, \ f = 6375, \ f_u = 1034$
 $S = 0.0000074, \ f = 914, \ f_u = 864$
 $S = 0.0000032, \ f = 902, \ f_u = 866$
 $S = 0.00000054, \ f = 900, \ f_u = 868$

finally yielding the solution

$$x_1 = 289.7, x_2 = 293.2, x_3 = 285.3 \qquad (6.9)$$

with

$$M = \begin{bmatrix} 1 & -0.5087 & -0.0718 \\ -0.05 & 1 & -0.0657 \\ -0.2776 & -0.5282 & 1 \end{bmatrix} \quad (6.10)$$

and with $\beta = 10$ the solution cannot be significantly improved.

If, on the other hand, only the first two of the latter searches with $\beta = 1$ are carried out, then a further two searches with $\beta = 10$, 100 and 1000, a similar solution is obtained, that is $x_1 = 295.8$, $x_2 = 297.7$ and $x_3 = 290.8$.

The solution, though approximate, is much closer to satisfying Equation 6.5 than the initial solution of Equations 6.1, that is $x_1 = 200$, $x_2 = 400$, $x_3 = 200$ (in Table 6.1), and the method used here shows some promise.

Applying constraints to matrix problems

Equation 6.11 is a hypothetical input-output analysis problem with the constraint $x_1 = 0.3x_3$ imposed using the *Lagrange multiplier* method.

$$\begin{bmatrix} 1 & -0.2 & -0.1 & -0.05 & 1 \\ -0.3 & 1 & -0.2 & -0.1 & 0 \\ -0.4 & -0.3 & 1 & -0.2 & -0.3 \\ -0.5 & -0.3 & -0.4 & 1 & 0 \\ 1 & 0 & -0.3 & 0 & 0.000001 \end{bmatrix} \begin{Bmatrix} x_1 \\ x_2 \\ x_3 \\ x_4 \\ \lambda \end{Bmatrix} = \begin{Bmatrix} 1 \\ 7 \\ 12 \\ 17 \\ 0 \end{Bmatrix} \quad (6.11)$$

The inclusion of the extra row and column corresponding to the Lagrange multiplier λ presents no difficulty and Mohr's *small slack variable* $1/\beta$, $\beta = 10^6$, is included on the diagonal so that pivoting is not required by the solution routine (normally a zero appears in this position).

6. INPUT-OUTPUT ANALYSIS

Without this constraint the solution is $\{x\} = \{10, 20, 30, 40\}$, but with it we obtain (to 3 d.p.)

$$\{x\} = \{8.839, 19.448, 29.462, 39.039, 0.949\} \qquad (6.12)$$

and this satisfies the constraint to 5 d.p., i.e. it is satisfied to the accuracy imposed by β (note that β should be 2-3 d.p. less than the precision of the computation).

Now, however, the original equations are only satisfied approximately (we have in effect altered them), for example substituting the values of Equation 6.12 into the first we obtain

$$x_1 - 0.2x_2 - 0.1x_3 - 0.05x_4 = 0.051 \qquad (6.13)$$

not = 1 as required, so that the value of λ must be included as well to obtain the correct result. The degree of approximation, and in turn the severity of the constraints, is then indicated by the magnitude of the Lagrange multiplier(s).

Such problems can be written in the general form

$$\begin{bmatrix} S & G^T \\ G & -I_m/\beta \end{bmatrix} \begin{Bmatrix} x \\ \lambda \end{Bmatrix} = \begin{Bmatrix} q \\ q_c \end{Bmatrix} \qquad (6.14)$$

where G is a matrix of m constraint equations and I_m is a unit matrix of order m.

Using the second row of Equation 6.14 we can write

$$\{\lambda\} = \beta G\{x\} - \beta\{q_c\} \qquad (6.15)$$

and substituting this result into the first row of Equation 6.14 gives

$$[S + \beta G^T G]\{x\} = \{q\} + \beta G^T\{q_c\} \qquad (6.16)$$

and this λ–β *transformation* was discovered by Mohr (1985).

6. INPUT-OUTPUT ANALYSIS

Now β acts as a *penalty factor* (so that the small slack variables might be described as inverse penalty factors). These are the preferred means of imposing such constraints because the original matrix is not increased in size, instead being augmented by the *penalty matrix* $\beta\, G^T G$.

This penalty method is easy to program, in the present example reading in a constraint row 1, 0, -0.3, 0, 0, where note that the last entry is the RHS or 'load' value (corresponding to q_c in Equation 6.14).

Using the penalty method (again with $\beta = 10^6$) the solution of Equation 6.12 is again obtained but there is no Lagrangian multiplier value to remind us of the degree of approximation (in relation to the unconstrained original equations), but if we calculate

$$\beta\,(x_1 - 0.3 x_3) = 0.949 \text{ (not zero)} \tag{6.17}$$

we see that that an implicit Lagrange multiplier value is revealed (the same as that obtained in Equation 6.12).

As noted above, RHS values for the constraints must be given (as indeed is the case for Lagrange multiplier constraints) and, for example, constraints such as $x_1 = x_3 + 10$ are easily imposed, the solution to our example then being (this replacing the original constraint)

$$\{x\} = \{31.326,\ 25.549,\ 21.326,\ 48.858\} \tag{6.18}$$

Note that such constraints as the latter can be added to any matrix solution routine such as that given earlier by adding

$$\beta \begin{bmatrix} 1 & 0 & -1 & 0 \\ 0 & 0 & 0 & 0 \\ -1 & 0 & 1 & 0 \\ 0 & 0 & 0 & 0 \end{bmatrix} = 10\beta \begin{Bmatrix} 1 \\ 0 \\ -1 \\ 0 \end{Bmatrix} \tag{6.19}$$

to the reduced/problem (without row/column 5) problem of Equation 6.11, giving the same result as Equation 6.18 (given the same β).

6. INPUT-OUTPUT ANALYSIS

Then note that in the special case where we want to suppress a variable to zero (the most common *boundary condition* in physical problems) we simply add a large (penalty) factor to the diagonal location in the coefficient matrix corresponding to that variable [i.e. in position (3,3) if it is the third variable].

Finally a third way of enforcing matrix is constraints is *basis transformation* (the 'basis' in any problem being the set of variables used to model it). If, for example, we wish to enforce the constraint $x_2 = x_4$ in our example problem we use the transformation

$$\{x'\} = \begin{Bmatrix} x'_1 \\ x'_2 \\ x'_3 \\ x'_4 \end{Bmatrix} = \begin{bmatrix} 1 & 0 & 0 & 0 \\ 0 & 1 & 0 & -1 \\ 0 & 0 & 1 & 0 \\ 0 & 0 & 0 & 1 \end{bmatrix} \begin{Bmatrix} x_1 \\ x_2 \\ x_3 \\ x_4 \end{Bmatrix} = T\{x\}$$

(6.20)

to transform the problem variables, using the *congruent transformation*

$$T^T S T \{x\} = \{q\}$$
(6.21)

to transform the coefficient matrix to that for the new variables.

Basis transformation is much used by Mohr's *method of nested interpolations* for *finite element* formulation to transform a *global* set of element variables to a more convenient *local* set corresponding to a known (convenient) interpolation.

The following program can be used to demonstrate all three constraint methods described above:

6. Input-Output Analysis

```
5 REM Lagrange Multiplier, Penalty & Basic constraints
10 DIM C(20, 20), V(20), G(10, 20), F(20)
15 a$ = "####": B$ = "########.###"
20 DIM T(20, 20), S(20, 20): B = 100000
30 RESTORE 420
40 READ NV, NC, NS, IB
50 FOR I = 1 TO NV: FOR J = 1 TO NV
60 READ C(I, J): NEXT: NEXT
70 FOR I = 1 TO NV: READ V(I): NEXT
80 FOR I = 1 TO NC: FOR J = 1 TO NV
90 READ G(I, J): NEXT: READ F(I): NEXT
100 IF IB = 0 THEN 160
110 FOR I = 1 TO NV: FOR J = 1 TO NV: READ T(I, J)
120 S(I, J) = C(I, J): NEXT: NEXT
130 FOR I = 1 TO NV: FOR J = 1 TO NV: C(I, J) = 0
140 FOR K = 1 TO NV: C(I, J) = C(I, J) + S(I, K) * T(K, J)
150 NEXT: NEXT: NEXT
160 FOR I = 1 TO NV: FOR K = 1 TO NC
170 V(I) = V(I) + B * G(K, I) * F(K): NEXT: NEXT
180 FOR I = 1 TO NV: FOR J = 1 TO NV
190 FOR K = 1 TO NC
200 C(I, J) = C(I, J) + G(K, I) * G(K, J) * B: NEXT K
210 NEXT J: NEXT I
220 FOR K = 1 TO NS
230 READ N, SP
240 FOR I = 1 TO NV
250 C(N, I) = 0: V(I) = V(I) - SP * C(I, N)
260 C(I, N) = 0: NEXT I
270 V(N) = SP: C(N, N) = 1: NEXT
280 FOR I = 1 TO NV: X = C(I, I): V(I) = V(I) / X
300 FOR J = I + 1 TO NV: C(I, J) = C(I, J) / X: NEXT
320 FOR K = 1 TO NV
330 IF K = I THEN GOTO 370
340 X = C(K, I): V(K) = V(K) - X * V(I)
350 FOR J = I + 1 TO NV
360 C(K, J) = C(K, J) - X * C(I, J): NEXT J
370 NEXT K
380 NEXT I
390 PRINT "Node     Value"
400 FOR I = 1 TO NV
410 PRINT USING a$; I; : PRINT USING B$; V(I): NEXT
```

6. INPUT-OUTPUT ANALYSIS

```
420 DATA 5,1,0,1
430 DATA 1,-.2,-.1,-.05,1
440 DATA -.3,100000,-.2,-.1,0
450 DATA -.4,-.3,1,-.2,-1
460 DATA -.5,-.3,-.4,1,0
470 DATA 1,0,-1,0,.000001    : REM L CONSTRAINT X1 = X3
480 DATA 1,7,12,17,0
490 DATA 1,-1,0,0,0,0  : REM PENALTY CONSTRAINT X1 = X2
500 DATA 1,0,0,0,0     : REM BASIS TRANS. MATRIX For X2 = X4
510 DATA 0,1,0,-1,0
520 DATA 0,0,1,0,0
530 DATA 0,0,0,1,0
540 DATA 0,0,0,0,1
```

The data is for the problem of Equation 6.11 and line 420 = 5 equations, 1 penalty constraint, no *specified (boundary)* values for the variables (if any these would be the last data lines, being read in line 230). The solution routine is Gauss-Mohr reduction, Gauss reduction modified for *direct solution* to operate only to the right of pivot and on the right side (i.e. the inverse matrix is not formed).

As noted above the penalty method is preferable to and equivalent to the Lagrange multiplier method (first proved by Mohr), whilst the basis transformation method is generally used for *transforming*, not constraining, variables.

Indeed trying to use all three methods at once and using the 'BT' method does not give the same results as for the other two methods because, in Equation 6.20, for example, it does not effectively *eliminate* variables from the solution (as the other methods do) but 'rescales' them'. At this point only some attention to the penalty method is recommended, and particularly the 'big number on the diagonal' method of suppressing variables to zero.

6. INPUT-OUTPUT ANALYSIS

Finite element IOA models

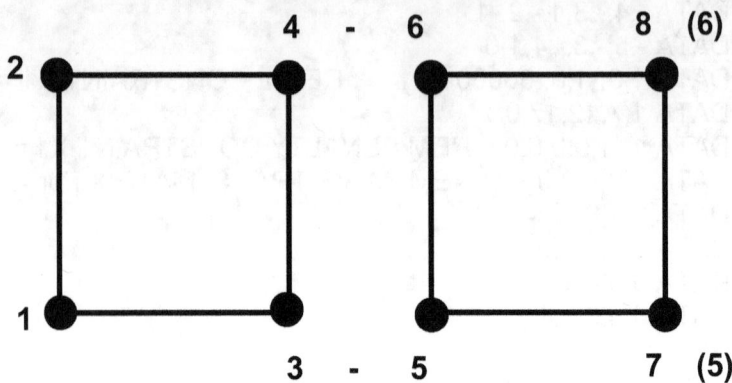

Figure 6.1. Two element system for IOA.

Here we see two 'elements' with four 'nodes'.
For the first element the following IOA equation applies:

$$\begin{bmatrix} 1 & -0.2 & -0.1 & -0.05 \\ -0.3 & 1 & -0.2 & -0.1 \\ -0.4 & -0.3 & 1 & -0.2 \\ -0.5 & -.3 & -0.4 & 1 \end{bmatrix} \begin{Bmatrix} x_1 \\ x_2 \\ x_3 \\ x_4 \end{Bmatrix} = \begin{Bmatrix} 1 \\ 7 \\ 12 \\ 17 \end{Bmatrix}$$

For the second the foregoing equation in symmetric form, with the below diagonal entries made equal to those above, is used.

The following listing is of a program which uses Gauss reduction to solve both symmetric and unsymmetric banded matrix problems.

Line 30 sets number of nodes per element (NCN) and the length of the band width to the left of the pivot (NM), that is *exclusive* half band width NBW, where half band width = (max. node no. difference in any element) X NDF, here with NDF = 1. For symmetric problems set NM = 0 and for unsymmetric problems set NM ≥ 1 (its value is calculated in line 40).

6. Input-Output Analysis

Following data lines give the node numbers for each element followed by its IOA matrix.

```
10 REM Band Solution Routine For I/O Analysis
20 DIM EM(6, 6), S(80, 41), R(41), Q(80), NN(10, 6)
30 RESTORE 500: NCN = 4: nm = 1
40 READ NP, NE, NBW: IF nm > 0 THEN nm = NBW
50 FOR I = 1 TO NP: READ Q(I): NEXT: REM Read loads
60 FOR N = 1 TO NE
70 FOR J = 1 TO NCN: READ NN(N, J): NEXT
REM Read element data
80 FOR I = 1 TO NCN: FOR J = 1 TO NCN
90 READ EM(I, J): NEXT: NEXT
100 FOR I = 1 TO NCN: NR = NN(N, I)
110 FOR J = 1 TO NCN: NC = NN(N, J)
120 NCB = NC - NR + nm + 1: IF NR > NC AND nm = 0 THEN 140
130 S(NR, NCB) = S(NR, NCB) + EM(I, J)
140 NEXT: NEXT
150 NEXT N
160 FOR L = 1 TO NP: REM ##### start reduction loop
170 NDIF = NP - L + 1: IF NDIF > NBW THEN LIM = NBW + 1
180 LIM = LIM - 1
190 XK = 1 / S(L, nm + 1): Q(L) = Q(L) * XK
200 FOR J = 1 TO LIM: IA = L + J: JA = nm + 1 - J: IF nm = 0 THEN IA = L
IF nm = 0 THEN JA = J + 1
210 IF JA < 1 THEN 220
R(J) = S(IA, JA): REM Collect row multipliers
220 NEXT
230 FOR J = 2 TO LIM + 1: S(L, J + nm) = S(L, J + nm) * XK: NEXT: REM Row/pivot
240 FOR I = 1 TO LIM: NR = L + I: NR = L + I
250 IF R(I) = 0 THEN 290
LC = nm - I + 2: IF nm = 0 THEN LC = 1
NC = LC + LIM
260 FOR J = LC TO NC: JP = J + I
270 S(NR, J) = S(NR, J) - S(L, JP) * R(I): NEXT
REM Row subtraction
280 Q(NR) = Q(NR) - R(I) * Q(L)
290 NEXT I
300 NEXT L: REM ##### end reduction loop
```

6. INPUT-OUTPUT ANALYSIS

```
310 FOR L = NP TO 1 STEP -1
320 IF LIM < NBW THEN LIM = LIM + 1
330 FOR J = 1 TO LIM: JA = J + 1 + nm
340 Q(L) = Q(L) - S(L, JA) * Q(L + J): NEXT: NEXT
REM Back substitution
350 FOR I = 1 TO NP: PRINT I, Q(I): NEXT
360 END
500 DATA 8,2,3
510 DATA 1,7,12,17,1,7,12,17
520 DATA 1,2,3,4
530 DATA 1,-.2,-.1,-.05
540 DATA -.3,1,-.2,-.1
550 DATA -.4,-.3,1,-.2
560 DATA -.5,-.3,-.4,1
570 DATA 5,6,7,8
580 DATA 1,-.2,-.1,-.05
590 DATA -.2,1,-.2,-.1
600 DATA -.1,-.2,1,-.2
610 DATA -.05,-.1,-.2,1
```

The data appended in lines 500 - 610 to the program is for problem of Fig. 12.2 with the two elements separate and Table 12.3 shows the results for this as case (a). In case (b) NM = 0 is specified (in line 30) and the element matrices are assumed symmetric (and treated accordingly) so that the solutions are the same four numbers.

In case (c) the node pairs 3,5 and 4,6 are merged and nodes 7,8 become 5,6, so that the node number set for element 2 is 3,4,5,6 and NBW = 3 still. Combining the 'loads' at the merged nodes we have $q_3 = 12$ and $q_4 = 24$. The data for this case is as follows (note that there NBW is the *inclusive* value, that is greater by 1 than in the program above).

```
1000 DATA 6,2,4
1005 DATA 1,7,13,24,12,17
1010 DATA 1,2,3,4
1020 DATA 1,-.2,-.1,-.05
1030 DATA -.3,1,-.2,-.1
1040 DATA -.4,-.3,1,-.2
1050 DATA -.5,-.3,-.4,1
```

6. INPUT-OUTPUT ANALYSIS

```
1060 DATA 3,4,5,6
1115 DATA 1,-.2,-.1,-.05
1120 DATA -.2,1,-.2,-.1
1130 DATA -.1,-.2,1,-.2
1140 DATA -.05,-.1,-.2,1
```

The results are, of course, quite different but note that with overlapping elements two diagonal entries will be two, not one as usual.

Table 6.1. Solutions for the system of Figure 6.1.

Node	(a)	(b)	(c)	(d)
1	10.00	7.12	6.90	25.51
2	20.00	14.76	14.90	45.47
3	30.00	20.24	16.85	93.24
4	40.00	22.88	24.63	121.74
5	7.12	7.12	23.62	54.62
6	14.76	14.76	25.03	44.76
7	20.24	20.24	-	
8	22.88	22.88	-	

Altering these to one, the result in case (d), now very different indeed, and it appears that case (c), in fact, is the appropriate solution for the overlapping element case.

This was confirmed by applying the constraints $x_3 = x_5$, $x_4 = x_6$ to the 8 node problem (case (a)) using penalty factors when exactly the same results as case (c) are obtained. Here $\beta \geq 10^4$ and 14 dp computation was used. With 8 dp computation and $\beta = 10^5$ the results are similar but less so with $\beta = 10^6$, illustrating that we require β about 3 'places' less than the precision of computation.

It is also confirmed by using the data in lines 1000+ above, where the two element matrices have been summed manually, when NCN = 6 must be set at the start of the program. Again the results of case (c) in Table 6.1 are obtained.

6. INPUT-OUTPUT ANALYSIS

References

Cunningham, BM, Loren, AN, Bazley JD, *Accounting: Information for Business Decisions*, Dryden Press, Orlando FL, 2000.

Caves RE, Frankel JA, Jones RW, *World Trade and Payments, An Introduction*, Scott Foresman/Little Brown, Glenview IL, 1990.

Hogarth R, Makridakis S, Forecasting and planning: an evaluation, *Management Science* 87 (1981) 115-138.

Klein, L.R., Pauly, P. and Voison, P. The world economy - a global model. *Perspectives in Computing*, vol. 2, no. 2, 1982.

Leontief WW, *The Structure of the American Economy*, 1919-1939, 2nd edn., OUP, Fair Lawn NJ, 1951.

Mohr GA, Numerical procedures for input-output analysis, *Applied Mathematics & Computation* 101 (1999) 89-98.

Mohr GA, Caffin DA, Penalty factors, Lagrange multipliers and basis transformation in the finite element method, *Trans IE Aust*, CE25, pp 174-180, 1985.

Mohr GA, *The Finite Element Method for Solids, Fluids, and Optimization,* OUP, Oxford, 1992.

Theil H, Boot JCG, Kloek T, *Operations Research and Quantitative Economics*, McGraw-Hill, NY, 1965.

Waud, RN, *Microeconomics*, 3rd edn, Harper & Row, New York, NY 1986.

Vernon, J. *Macoeconomics*. Dryden Press, Hinsdale IL, 1980.

Wonnacott P, Wonnacott R, *Economics*, McGraw-Hill, New York 1979.

Chapter 7

SUPPLY AND DEMAND INVERTED

> *The science* [economics] *hangs like a gathering fog in a valley, a fog which begins nowhere and goes nowhere, an incidental, unmeaning inconvenience to passers-by.*
> H. G. Wells, *A Modern Utopia* (1905).

Turning S&D around

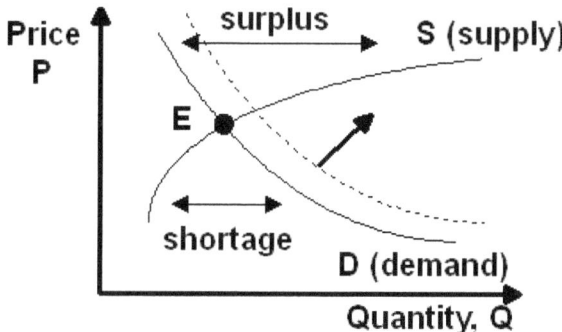

Figure 7.1. Traditional supply and demand curves.

The cornerstone of modern economics is the law of supply and demand. Some economics textbooks are so filled with obtuse S&D diagrams that they literally drive you mad.

Figure 7.1 shows typical supply and demand curves for which it is frequently assumed that there is *perfect competition*, that is there are many buyers and sellers and none are able to influence the price individually. Then the result is called a *competitive market*.

7. Supply and Demand Inverted

Here the supply goes up as the price goes up because the supplier is more motivated to produce more goods. The S curve, therefore, is drawn from the point of view of the *supplier*.

The demand curve, on the other hand, goes down as the price goes down because with a greater quantity of goods available competition forces the price down (or conversely shortages result in increased prices). Hence the D curve is drawn from the point of view of the buyer.

The two curves intersect at point E, the equilibrium point at which supply equals demand.

That economists stick to the old fashioned S&D model of Figure 7.1 is a sure indication that they are behind the times. The model of Figure 7.1 applies well enough to agricultural or mineral products, for example, but not too heavily marketed products such Coke or McDonald's.

For these there is really no such thing as a shortage in supply, but, if there were to be such a shortage it would certainly reduce demand. No, these products have *created* a demand by using mass production to reduce costs and then advertising heavily.

The car industry, however, is perhaps the classic example. Australia, for example, is said to have begun to become 'motorized' in the mid 1950s. Before that relatively few people had cars and public transport was used to commute to work and school and holidays were taken by using buses, trains and, to a lesser extent, airplanes to get there.

Now, thanks to marketing, just about everybody has a car and, for example, dad parks his all day at the station and takes the train to the city to work, and mum uses hers to go shopping and pick up young children from the nearest school.

It was in the mid 1950s, however, that the world's population needed to reach a plateau fairly quickly. Then we wouldn't have such sprawling megacities and we wouldn't all need cars and the world wouldn't be on the verge of rapidly running out of oil and badly depleting many other vital resources.

7. SUPPLY AND DEMAND INVERTED

Inverse law of supply and demand

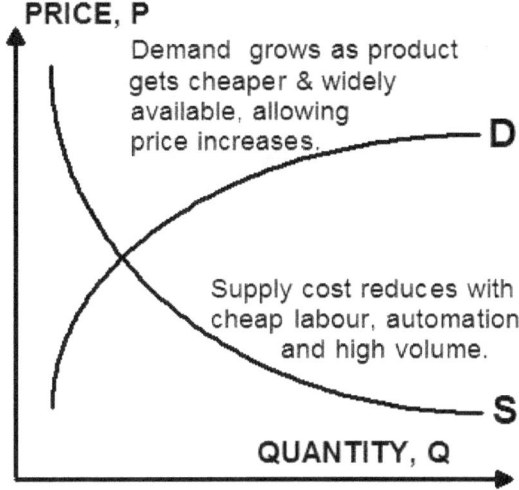

Inverse Law of Supply & Demand

Figure 7.2. Inverse law of supply and demand, Mohr (2012, 2012b, 2014, 2017, 2018).

The cornerstone of modern economics is the law of supply and demand. In this the supply curve goes up as price increases, motivating greater production, and the demand curve goes down with increasing production, greater availability of goods decreasing their price. The two curves intersect at the equilibrium point at which supply equals demand.

The original 'D down' form applied OK in Adam Smith's day (1723 – 1790) but for today's global market S & D curves should often be the reverse, as shown in Figure 7.2, because:

(a) Economies of scale, use of casual labour, cheap labour in developing countries, etc. reduce cost.

(b) Mass marketing tends to sell as much as is produced.

The original 'D down' form still applies sometimes, for example in the case of food and commodities such as oil:

The first law of economics is that when the price goes up, consumption goes down. This is a divine law.
You cannot change it.
Sheikh Ahmed Yamani, Saudi Arabian Politician referring to OPEC's raising of oil prices in the early 1970s.

7. Supply and Demand Inverted

In modern global markets in which products are mass produced and heavily marketed the 'reversed' S&D model is that which applies and the massive growth in China's economy in recent decades is testament to this.

Some years ago the PC might have been a good example. The first microcomputers were tiny affairs suitable only for hobbyists but Clive Sinclair brought their price down to the point that they were affordable as toys for children.

Then the first PCs suitable for business purposes, however, were quite expensive at first. Along came the IBM 'clone' from Asia, however, and that brought the price of PCs down to the affordable levels we still see today for 'bottom of the range' but extremely powerful PCs with dazzling clock speeds compared to those of yore.

Conclusions

One great mistake made by economists is that they don't see that S&D diagrams should have two alternative forms, depending upon whether:
(a) One is dealing with agricultural or mineral products prone to supply variations depending on such factors as the weather or discovery of new deposits.
(b) One is dealing with nonessential mass produced products for which large scale production reduces unit costs and for which the demand is stimulated by advertising.

References

Mohr GA, *The Pretentious Persuaders,* Horizon Publishing Group, Sydney (2012, 2014 – 2nd edition).

Mohr GA, *The Doomsday Calculation,* Xlibris, Sydney (2012).

Mohr GA, *Elementary Thinking for the 21st Century,* Xlibris, Sydney (2014).

Mohr G.A., *The Brainwashed, From Consumer Zombies to Islamism and Jihad,* Inspiring Publishers, Canberra, 2016.

7. Supply and Demand Inverted

Mohr GA, *The Scientific MBA*, 5th ed., *Balboa Press*, Bloomington IN (2017).

Mohr GA, *Elementary Thinking for Modern Management*, Amazon-Kindle (2018).

7. Supply and Demand Inverted

Chapter 8

GLOBALIZATION

> *Global democratic capitalism is as unrealizable a condition as worldwide communism.*
> John Gray, *False Dawn* (1998).

Distribution models

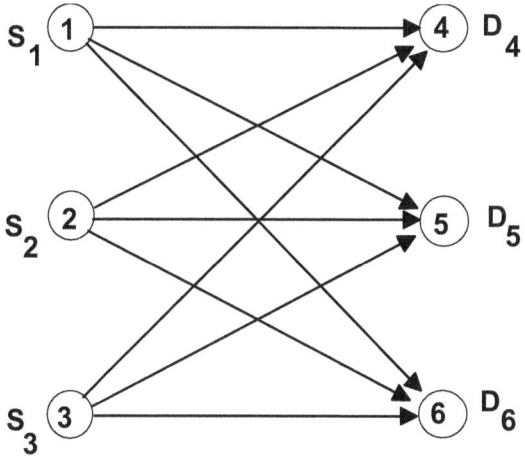

Figure 8.1. Distribution network.

Figure 8.1 shows a distribution network with 3 supply points and 3 demand points. The flows for these 6 points and the *unit costs* of shipping one item on each of the nine routes are given in Table 8.1 (Mohr, 2017).

8. Globalization

Table 8.1. Distribution problem data.

Unit costs			Supplies
5	10	10	110 [1]
20	30	20	160 [2]
10	20	30	150 [3]
140 [4]	200 [5]	80 [6]	
Demands			

The optimum network can be determined using Linear Programming (Budnick et al., 1977) and this gives the minimum total transportation cost $T = 6,700$ and has only five routes with flows:

$15 = 110$, $25 = 80$, $26 = 80$, $34 = 140$, $35 = 10$

and the number of non-zero route flows = (# supply points + # demand points) - 1, as is always the case in this type of problem.

The problem can also be modeled using the Finite Element Method (Mohr 1999, 2000) and this has the advantage that day-to-day variations in any network can be modeled.

In FEM only small '2 by 2' matrices based on a variation of Ohm's law for DC networks are needed to represent each route or 'element' in Figure 8.1, and the element matrices are 'assembled' to form a 'system matrix' in a matrix equation like Equation 6.2. This equation is then solved to determine the 'potential' at each of the supply and demand points, from which the flows in each route are then calculated.

This approach has also been extended to model traffic flows in road networks (Mohr, 2005).

Such FEM models are an essential tool for modeling the large distribution networks of today's large transnational companies. Even the simple example of Figure 8.1 reminds us of the importance of having more than one production operation and thence supply point to feed a global market.

That optimizing the network of Figure 8.1 eliminates 4 routes, emphasizes that globalization should be limited to involve only the most efficient and profitable arrangements.

8. Globalization

The upside of globalization

The so-called a "neo-liberal" approach to globalization is based on laissez-faire economics and thus holds that globalization will yield maximum gains when it is free of any regulation and subject only to market forces.

Globalization can also be claimed to be a boon to consumers because it increases the range of products available to them. Then, as consumer tastes around the world become more similar the potential sales for products marketed globally can only increase.

It also allows components of products such as PCs and aircraft to be manufactured in different countries.

Of most importance to management, global markets offer prospects of increased profits through higher sales volumes and thence economies of scale in production.

Capitalists also pursue globalization since it allows production facilities to be sited wherever costs are lowest and the profits greatest. Furthermore, global accounting practices enable prices and taxes to be calculated in ways that raise profits.

Finally, global connections themselves (tele-communications, electronic finance, and so on) create major opportunities for profit making.

Concerns about globalization

The major concerns raised by globalization include protection of local jobs and the environment and many see the need for government policies that can restrict global flows when necessary.

In several countries there have also been objections to the role of US 'cultural imperialism' in the globalization process.

Nationalists see globalization as a threat to economic prosperity, cultural heritage, democracy, the environment, and social welfare.

Socialists regard capitalism in any form as evil, and globalized capitalization as even more so.

8. Globalization

Since the mid-1990's the 'anti-globalization movement' has held regular mass protests against global companies, the International Monetary Fund, and prominent politicians whom they associate with globalization.

Neo-colonialism in developing countries

Former colonies of rich nations remain heavily linked to the First World in dependent relationship often termed 'neo-colonialism' (Bell & Hall, 1991). Reasons for this dependency include:

➤ International trade and investment policies usually favour the rich nations which, for example, often set tariffs to protect their own agricultural industries.

➤ Multinational companies are sometimes more powerful than Third World countries and establish factories using cheap labour, using the threat of withdrawal from the country to keep wages unreasonably low.

➤ Large sums of money lent to poor countries has left them with unpayable debt burdens which have undermined their economic growth.

➤ Western advertising of products such as tobacco and infant bottle milk formula has distorted consumption patterns in some poor countries and also caused long-term health problems.

➤ The high cost of Western arms cripples strife-torn countries in such places as Africa.

➤ The high cost of Western pharmaceutical products, for example for treating AIDS, adds another crippling burden to the fragile economies of poor countries in Africa.

Not surprisingly the former USSR was actively trying to encourage socialist governments in some poor countries in northern Africa in the 1970s and 1980s. The political situation in some of these countries remains unstable at the present time.

8. Globalization

Negative results in developed countries

Globalization has also had many negative impacts in developed countries, for example:

➢ Global efforts by Japanese manufacturers led to the demise of the UK motor bike industry in the 1950s.

➢ Likewise, foreign manufacturers put most of the UK car industry out of business during the 1960s and 1970s.

➢ In Australia manufacturers of radios, TVs and record players were put out of business by imports by the 1970s.

➢ Many smaller economies like that of Australia have 'gone along' with larger ones in floating their currencies. Dependent on commodities such as aluminium, iron and uranium as it is, however, Australia's economy would have been much better served over the last 30 years if its currency had been pegged (Caves et al., 1990).

➢ The combined French and Chinese companies Lonovo-Galanz began to dominate the world market for 'cheap' microwave ovens in the 1990s. The Chinese have now taken over Lonovo and also IBMs PC business.

➢ Now the US car industry is in trouble with GM and Ford suffering large losses whilst the Toyota Corolla is now the largest selling car in the USA.

In Australia we have General Motors Holden, Ford and Toyota still operating, Mitsubishi having left several years ago, but the government has to regularly 'prop up' GMH and Ford whose futures in Australia look uncertain.

In addition, however, we shall never be able to believe that it makes economic sense to ship cars from all over Europe and Asia to Australia. The unit costs of shipping must be several thousands of dollars per car, a complete waste of money and, of course, precious oil. In addition, Japan gets its iron ore from Australia, making the economics of us importing cars from Japan completely ridiculous.

The same applies to countless other products. Sure, it's nice to be drink some different beers from time to time, but it can't make good socio-economic or environmental sense.

8. Globalization

Privatization and globalization

An ongoing process in the West has been privatization of government run public utilities such as public transport and electricity, gas and water supply. Along with this the practice of outsourcing road building, recruitment and other activities has long been on the increase.

Some of these businesses are a licence to print money because they are essential services so that they *can't* go out of business. When the private company gets into trouble they are invariably bailed out by the government.

The multinational companies that persuade countries to sell off their assets invariably sack a good proportion of the work force as soon as possible so that the government has to foot the bill for yet more people on the dole.

The negative effects of globalization are felt nowhere more than in the clothing industry where brands such as Nike set up factories in Mexico, China and other poorer regions of the world to make use of their cheap labour that will work under appalling conditions.

Indeed, everywhere you look privatization and globalization are having negative effects and taking us back to Dickensian conditions and lifestyles.

In Australia half of the phone company Telstra was privatized several years ago, and the other half was sold off a few years ago. Much of these floats were taken up by overseas companies. The result was the loss of much government revenue so that, once again, new taxes such as a GST and a carbon tax were introduced.

As things stand there is little left for the government to sell except its soul, if it has one that is, which much, if not most, of the public doubts.

Such sales have retired a good deal of government debt but, with almost no tariff protection remaining for local industry, foreign debt has begun to climb yet again. But in the future there will be nothing left to sell and we shall regress amongst the nations to what might be termed a 'second world' status, if we have not reached that point already that is.

8. Globalization

The future

According to Hilmer and Donaldson (1996), just as several car companies amalgamated respectively into one in the UK and three in the USA, the trend since the 1990s has been for international amalgamations, for example GM with SAAB and Ford with Mazda. After the GFC the US government had to prop up GM and Chrysler and GM sold off SAAB.

They conclude that, while some large companies may have to shrink in order to remain afloat, others will take their place because only large corporations can effectively compete globally.

They also conclude, however, that there will always be a place for new, small companies to start up, and also for small companies with a niche market.

The author sees the balance of power in the world moving from the 'USA-UK and friends' alliance to China, India and Russia, interestingly enough three countries with common borders. Should they choose to form a trade bloc it would represent almost half the world's population, especially if it included former USSR member countries such as Kazakhstan and India's neighbour Pakistan.

As already noted, smaller and poorer third-world countries in Africa and elsewhere have gained nothing from globalization but lost much.

As the author wrote in 2005 (Mohr, 2012):

"Of most importance, however, is the question of whether serious economic collapses in major players in the global market could lead to a worldwide downturn comparable to the Great Depression circa 1930.

It requires little reflection to conclude that the combined effects of the energy crisis, global food shortages, the spread of new diseases, and ongoing wars and terrorism, could indeed trigger such a global economic depression."

Since he wrote those words we have had the Global Financial Crisis or GFC of 2008+ and the effects of this are still being felt with interest rates in most countries remaining much lower than they were before the GFC.

8. Globalization

References

Bell R, Hall R, *Impact: Contemporary Issues & Global Problems,* The Jacaranda Press, Brisbane (1991).

Budnick FS, Mojena R, Vollmann TE, *Principles of Operations Research for Management,* Irwin, Homewood IL 1977.

Hilmer FG, Donaldson L, *Management Redeemed: Debunking the fads that undermine corporate performance,* The Free Press, Sydney (1996).

Mohr, GA, Finite element modeling of distribution problems, Applied Mathematics & Computation 105 (1999) 69-76.

Mohr, GA, Optimization of primal and dual network models of distribution, Computer Methods in Applied Mechanics & Engineering 188 (2000) 135-144.

Mohr GA, Finite element modeling and optimization of traffic flow networks, *Transportmetrica* 1 (2005) 151-159.

Mohr GA, *The Doomsday Calculation,* Xlibris, Sydney (2012).

Mohr GA, *The Scientific MBA,* Balboa Press, Bloomington IN (2017).

Theil H, Boot JCG, Kloek T, Operations Research and Quantitative Economics, McGraw-Hill, NY, 1965.

Chapter 9

CURRENT ISSUES

> *Oil, despite its far reaching importance, is a transient phenomenon, whose finite life span will end, sooner or later.* Sheikh Ahmed Yamani, referring to OPEC's raising of oil prices in 1973, q. n *Arabia: The Islamic World Review* (October 1981).

The energy crisis

The supposedly strongest economies consume the most energy and there is a desperate need for considerable reductions in *energy intensity,* that is, in the amount of energy required to produce one unit of GNP.

A 1993 World Energy Council publication suggested an average world figure for efficiency of energy use as 3 to 3.5%. In Western Europe and Japan it is 4 to 5% and in the USA only 2%.

A major problem is that renewable energy sources are, on average, about twice as costly as conventional sources such as coal and oil. This is a difficult burden for industry to bear in a highly competitive global market and some have suggested that householders should bear the brunt of such increased energy costs in order to keep a nation's industries internationally competitive.

With oil set to run out in only 20 years and natural gas in about 50, however, the energy crisis is one that we have never experienced before in all our history. Nations may not be merely faced with the problem of remaining economically competitive, they are more likely to face stalling production and economic collapse as energy supplies dwindle.

9. Current Issues

Massive deficits

Many nations import large amounts of oil from oil-producing countries and do not sell them anything in return, resulting in massive balance of payment deficits. As Adam Smith puts it in *Paper Money* (1981), the two 'oil shocks' engineered by OPEC in 1973 resulted in "the greatest transfer of wealth in world history." They also caused decreased production and increased unemployment in industrialized nations. Speaking of the USA, Smith adds:

> *The threat of the Club's* [OPEC] *control is not the inconvenience of waiting in gas lines;*
> *it is that we are issuing blank checks on the country for a product that burns up in the atmosphere.*
> *We assume we can go right on issuing them.*
> *We have already issued the checks for Illinois, North Carolina, Arkansas, Wisconsin, and Georgia.*

The USA also has the problem we like to call the 'Keynes hole', remembering that Keynes said that war was like digging a huge hole and pouring money into it.

Yet again it is increasing already massive deficits by keeping large military forces and bases in Iraq, Afghanistan and other parts of the world. The result is that the USA has already breached World Bank limits on borrowing and is now in serious economic trouble.

The British used to joke that they were still paying off the Napoleonic wars. The USA has now also found itself in that situation, with England the USA now the most heavily indebted nations in history.

Many countries have followed down the American path and reduced mounting deficits by selling government infrastructure assets such as electricity, gas, water utilities as well as airlines and railways.

Often the companies running these once public assets are very quick to ask for government handouts if they have trouble making a profit whereas, under government control most of these assets made large profits.

9. Current Issues

One reason for this is that the original government utilities were monopolies which were split up and sold to a number of private operators, inevitably involving considerable duplication of running costs.

These countries, of which Australia and the UK are examples, are still accumulating deficits and will not in the future have anything left to sell off to help reduce them.

Resource depletion

The energy crisis really began with the OPEC oil shocks of 1973 and, as quoted at the start of this chapter, Sheikh Ahmed Yamani told us so at the time. Certainly, OPEC's action sparked greater efforts to find new oil deposits, for example those in the North Sea, and this bought us a little more time. Now the time is finally running out as we drill and dig deeper and deeper for coal and oil.

In addition, of course, many other resources are being depleted, including many vital minerals (Mohr, 2014; Mohr et al. 2018). Shortages of these will push up costs in many industries.

Food supplies in some parts of the world, at least, have been grossly inadequate, and millions still die each year of starvation or malnutrition. Millions of other undernourished people also fall victim to resurgent diseases such as malaria and newcomers such as AIDS.

Optimists say that we are capable of producing more food but we are fast losing arable land to desert as a result of intensive agriculture, pollution, mining, settlements and global warming.

Fish stocks were seriously depleted decades ago and are in danger of almost disappearing altogether.

Crops are endangered by the increasing resistance of insects and fungi to the chemicals used to control them.

Water supplies are inadequate for most of the world's population and elsewhere being increasingly stretched by droughts which may be the result of global warming and have been long enough to become the norm and not the exception.

9. Current Issues

Costs of pollution

With the onset of global warming various schemes for pollution taxes have been proposed. These will place an economic impost on key industries in many countries and reduce their competitiveness in increasingly tough international markets.

A positive outcome of such taxes might be that they should encourage industries to gradually switch to alternative cleaner energy sources. Nevertheless, this is certain to result in increased costs for the long term.

Much industrial pollution, however, is not produced by energy use but by the use of dangerous and often toxic materials. In such cases inevitable cost increases will have to be borne by industry and passed on to consumers.

For some countries highly reliant on relatively abundant coal reserves such as the USA and Australia there was considerable reluctance to sign the Kyoto protocol for greenhouse gas emission. Put simply, this is because they fear that the costs associated in reducing their emissions will lead to an increase in their already growing national debts.

This underlines the fact that the combined problems such as overpopulation, excessive consumption and resource depletion that face us do indeed threaten us with economic disasters.

The global market

Occasionally there are protests against globalization, presumably because of the affect they have on local industries and thence employment.

As with most things the overpaid CEOs of big business do, setting up factories in such countries as China and India to take advantage of cheap labour is only a short-term expedient to improve the company's bottom line and thence further inflate their massive personal incomes.

9. Current Issues

In the long term they can only do damage to their own country, perhaps permanent damage. The USA is a case in point because, increasingly, it looks certain that China will soon become the world's largest economy, displacing the USA from that position.

Russia too may make a resurgence as it is the world's fifth largest oil producer and the world's largest producer of natural gas and thus looks likely to prosper in the growing global marketplace.

Generally, however, globalization is a bad thing from the point of view of most countries that have the potential to be relatively self-sufficient. This is because it cannot be cheaper, for example, for consumers in Australia to buy cars from all over Europe, Asia and other countries, as well as cars made locally. Indeed, the cost of shipping cars between countries that produce their own must be very costly and wasteful of the world's fast vanishing reserves of oil.

Unfortunately, thanks in part to tariffs on most imported cars having been reduced to 5%, whereas China had had tariffs of 15%, Australia's car industry has now vanished.

The same questions of intercontinental distribution costs and economies of scale apply to most products, whether they be food or manufactured products.

There must, of course, always be a few highly specialized products with which certain countries have a competitive advantage which has been maintained over a long period of time.

Is continuing growth possible?

Economists include in their never ending and usually meaningless 'econobabble' statements that their country's economy has grown by some small percentage during the last year or lesser period (Mohr, 2014b).

Never mind that the country may be running up a massive debt or producing far more pollution than it should, also a cost to be borne by future generations.

In any case, they should be talking of net growth, that is, growth after inflation of the currency is taken into account.

9. Current Issues

It is doubtful that continuing net growth in the economies of developed nations is sensible, worthwhile or even possible.

In fact, diminishing resources are certain to limit economic growth throughout the world before long. One reason for this is that, as population grows so too must production, and provision of the infrastructure for this growth of production in turn further depletes diminishing resources.

Costs of terrorism

The massive cost of war has been mentioned earlier in this chapter. With it may go even greater costs of reconstruction, much of it often born by the invading country, as is the case now in Afghanistan.

In recent years terrorism throughout the world has resulted in enormous increases in spending on security by governments and industry, particularly the airlines and other industries associated with travel and tourism.

Terrorists have frequently blown up vital oil pipelines.

It cannot be long before they infect water and food supplies.

This would result in massive costs to governments and industry. Indeed, if it came to the point that water supplies to major cities were doubtful the very survival of those cities would be in doubt.

Collapse?

Many countries in the world today are in extreme economic difficulty and rely on support from richer nations. It seems inevitable that their plight will become worse as donor nations themselves slide deeper and deeper into debt and, perhaps, economic collapse.

With economic trouble looming for the most affluent countries which consume the most energy and other resources, the military and economic roles they play in the world must wane, perhaps resulting in greater strife in troubled areas of the globe such as Africa, the Middle East, parts of Asia, and South America.

9. Current Issues

Thus, it seems likely that political unrest, terrorism and war will actually increase from already unacceptable levels.

One reason for our economic troubles is the incompetence and economic BS or 'ecobabble' about issues like unemployment and interest rates. Continuing high unemployment rates in the West, however, are in line with Karl Marx's proposal that unemployment rates of about 5% are just what capitalist systems want to keep wage rates down and thence increase profits (Sweezy, 1946).

As for interest rates, contrary to what we are always told by idiots, increasing interest rates *increases* inflation, as one should expect, and a comprehensive proof of this was given in Chapter 5.

Chapter 7 also proposes a 'reverse' law of supply and demand for manufactured products because the original law of supply and demand really only applies to food and other commodities.

China's economic boom

Some believe that China has, at least in effect, reversed the Keynes multiplier effect (that increasing government spending involves a *multiplier effect* which results in a much larger increase in GNP). That is, they have allowed private capital from the major capitalist countries such as the US to stimulate their economy. The imported capital investment came from greedy American companies that set up in China to exploit their cheap labour and have helped kick-start China into an economic boom.

In addition, the Chinese government has supported over 20 major Chinese companies so that they could grow into major multinational operations, a practice more like the conventional Keynes effect.

The result has been that Chinese companies now dominate the global market for household electrical goods and have also became major players in the PC business and in the huge white goods business.

9. Current Issues

In addition, cheap Chinese clothing and $2+ shop products are sold globally and priced so low that nobody else can compete. In addition Chinese government companies now own, for example, much of Australia's electricity network.

Some of us remember that some Japanese products such as cars were viewed as being somewhat cheap and nasty in the mid 1960s. That certainly changed a great deal and their product quality in some areas is undoubtedly unsurpassable.

In the fullness of time the cheaper Chinese products will improve in quality and increase in price, further swelling their trade surplus with countries like the US.

The US is already seeing red (ink) about this and suggesting that China should devalue its currency which it pegs and does not float.

Pegging a currency, in fact, does have some advantages, for example that occasional adjustments, rather than constant daily fluctuations, tend to have more effect so that the government has much more control over its economy and importers and exporters have much greater certainty.

Australia floated its currency around 1970 but perhaps should not have:

If traded goods with prices determined exogenously on world markets constitute a large proportion of the economy, then exchange rate uncertainty translates into a high degree of uncertainty in the economy's overall price level. Such an economy may be too small and too open to have an independently floating currency.
Caves et al., *World Trade and Payments* (1990).

As for the 'econobabblers', they always sound like a record stuck in the same damaged groove when exchange rates alter significantly. If our currency goes down they say that it will be good for the economy because exports will be cheaper and will therefore increase in quantity. If it goes up they say that it will be good for the economy because exports will be dearer and earn us more money, neglecting to point out that the quantity of exports should be expected to fall.

In other words, they don't know what they are talking about.

References

Benham, F. Economics, 6th edn. Pitman, London, 1960.

Caves RE, Frankel JA, Jones RW, *World Trade and Payments: An Introduction,* Scott Foresman/Little Brown, Glenview IL (1990).

Clark, G. *In Fear of China.* Lansdown Press, Melbourne, 1972.

Mohr GA, *The Doomsday Calculation,* Xlibris, Sydney (2014).

Mohr GA, *The Pretentious Persuaders, A Brief History & Science of Mass Persuasion,* 2nd edn, Horizon Publishing Group, Sydney (2014b).

Mohr GA, *Elementary Thinking for the 21st Century,* Xlibris, Sydney (2014c).

Mohr GA, Fear E, *The Brainwashed: From Consumer Zombies to Islamism and Jihad,* Inspiring Publishers, Canberra (2016).

Mohr GA, *The Scientific MBA,* 5th ed., *Balboa Press,* Bloomington IN (2017).

Mohr GA, *Elementary Thinking for Modern Management,* Amazon-Kindle (2018).

Mohr GA, Mohr PE, Mohr RS, *The Population Explosion: The Problems, Solutions, and Prediction,* Amazon-Kindle (2018).

Smith A, *Paper Money,* Summit Books, New York (1981).

Sweezy PM, *The Theory of Capitalist Development*, Dennis Dobson, London (1946).

9. Current Issues

Chapter 10

KEY POLICY OBJECTIVES

> *It is tragically inevitable that, as human beings become over-abundant in relation to other resources, their marginal value diminishes and the dignity of human life deteriorates correspondingly. For the safeguard of the worth and sanctity of human life it is imperative that man does not become the cheapest of all commodities.*
> Carlo Cipolla,
> *The Economic History of World Population*, 6th edn (1974).

Dealing with the major issues

Given real democracy in government, and also in management, the question of the 'right objectives' for society remains. These should be self-evident and should not need to be believed by the gullible to have been blazed in stone by some god or other. Important, if not essential, objectives include:

[1] Population control.

As has been suggested by many, the world's population is at least twice that which is sustainable with any reasonable quality of life for all (Mohr, 2014; Mohr et al., 2018). Resources and strategies to humanely achieve this goal are long overdue. The silence of pompous leaders of governments and the church who have no real purpose other than self-aggrandizement on this issue has been culpable in the extreme.

10. Key Policy Objectives

Birth control programs have been introduced in a few of the poorest African countries, but much more needs to be done globally to educate people about the dangers of overpopulation and how to avoid unwanted pregnancies, and to provide the 'pill' and other birth control measures more widely, and to legalize abortion (and thus make it safer).

[2] Restriction of consumption.

We need to take urgent action to discourage, if not penalize, wasteful consumption. In a world where about half the population has insufficient food and unclean water it is absurd that in developed countries mindless people still have to have to have household pets which are often treated like royalty, *copying* a *fashion* that only originated in the 18th century in Europe. Indeed, in a saner society, people mindlessly walking their 'dog toys' about might be deemed insane.

[3] Resource conservation.

Measures are urgently needed to help conserve vital resources, particularly fast vanishing oil. The world has around 200 years of coal left and conservation of this too must be considered.

Thus energy conservation is of particularly importance. Gas guzzling cars have been tolerated far too long and the mindless executives that have pushed these should be penalized heavily.

High rise buildings with massive lighting and air conditioning requirements were not necessary not long ago and should not be necessary in the future.

In short, we do not need bigger and bigger bombs, airplanes, buildings, cars, TV screens and refrigerators and the industries that push things this way are run by megalomaniacs reminiscent of Adolf Hitler. It should be a crime to grossly waste precious resources and they should be stripped of their excessive salaries and wealth and sent to jail. As much as any drug dealer they are criminals.

10. Key Policy Objectives

[4] Renewable energy sources.
These need much accelerated research and implementation. It is only by a *combination* of the best available alternative and renewable energy sources that modern 'high-tech' society will survive to any extent.

[5] Pollution control.
Current efforts to limit pollution need to be much increased.

Industrial pollution remains excessive and more effective 'less toothless' environmental protection agencies are needed to see to it that industrial pollution is curtailed as far as possible and unwarranted offenders are penalized.

Cars with much smaller engines must rapidly become the norm to reduce their energy consumption and emissions.

Better technology to reduce emissions from the use of coal in industry and for power generation is urgently needed and must be developed and put in place as soon as possible.

Reduction of radioactive emission from the stacks of nuclear power plants must be achieved as a high priority, as must reduction of radioactive and thermal pollution of rivers and lakes produced by nuclear power plants.

[6] Reduction of greenhouse gas emissions.
As just discussed, pollution control will greatly reduce greenhouse gas emissions, for example from the burning of fossil fuels, particularly coal and oil.

The Kyoto protocol was a useful step but, deplorably, two of the main offenders on a per capita basis, the USA and Australia, refused to sign it. Now talk is that industry, not governments, should deal with the greenhouse problem. This is government abrogating its very purpose and any government so-doing should be forced out of office with delay.

Now that the world is aware of the fact that too much fat in the diet roughly doubles the incidence of cancer and cardiovascular disease a substantial reduction in our consumption of meat products should be encouraged.

10. Key Policy Objectives

Developments such as mad cow disease and the H5N1 strain of bird flu should also encourage reduction in meat consumption. Reduction of the size of livestock herds would then reduce methane emissions.

Deforestation should be curtailed with the utmost urgency and reforestation schemes widened in scope and accelerated to help restore the important carbon sink role that forests play in reducing CO_2 concentrations in the atmosphere.

[7] Environmental conservation.

Less intensive farming that causes less damage and pollution to the soil and rivers must become the norm in developed countries. This must be more careful with the use of fertilizers and pest control agents.

In the US and elsewhere rapidly depleting aquifers and other ground waters must be used less intensively.

As noted earlier, deforestation must be curtailed and reforestation increased.

We also need to reverse the trend to globalization centred around a few megacities with ever increasing urban areas around them linked by clogged freeways full of polluting cars commuting to and fro from non-productive jobs in front of PC screens in horrible high rise buildings at the centre of the city. This point is returned to later in the chapter.

[8] Prevention and control of disease.

Malaria is now more prevalent than ever before and kills a million or more people each year.

Half the world's population has insufficient food and unsafe water, resulting in epidemic levels of disease coupled with decreased resistance to them

An example is River Blindness which afflicts millions of children in Africa. A program of twice yearly vitamin A dosage is successfully curing this and halving the mortality rates in children.

AIDS reached epidemic proportions in Africa long ago. Now it is predicted to do likewise in Asia. Urgent action, for example educational programs, is needed to help reduce this threat.

10. Key Policy Objectives

[9] Economic well-being (for the community)

In the 1950s it was well-known that ZPG (zero population growth) was needed and unfortunately nobody gave effective voice to this fact.

The developed countries no longer need economic growth and, perhaps, a little zero economic growth (ZEG) might be tolerable. Certainly, however, in countries like the USA which consume far too much, ZEG should be a sensible objective.

The unrestrained madness of globalization and the laissez fair free market and monetarist approach to economics has been a failure and has brought us to the point of crisis as a result of excessive consumption not sufficiently mindful of resource depletion and pollution. Now we must pay the price.

To redress the critical situation responsible fiscal economic management is needed with greater government influence and ownership of essential services, and better and more timely 'tweaking' of government spending and interest rates, and other key economic variables. It would also help if economists understood the 'inverse' law of supply and demand for mass-produced manufactured goods (Figure 7.2) and that raising interest rates increases inflation, as proved in Chapter 5.

[10] Peace, not war.

Before it is too late we need to take unilateral measures to limit and prevent war. This should include reformation of the UN so that the USA, UK, Russia and China can no longer virtually control it and wage war with its approval, making a farce of the very title of the organization.

We need to ban land mines forthwith. Ditto nuclear and biochemical weapons, if not nearly all weapons. Sure, we will always need police and, therefore, armies to deal with contingencies of a larger scale.

The massive resources that continue to be wasted on weapons research and production, and armies and war, however, should be directed at *more urgent* priorities such as the starving and disease ridden millions in parts of Africa, Asia and South America.

10. Key Policy Objectives

Karl Marx said that *religion is the opiate of the people.* This is true with most key issues such as the overpopulation issue so culpably ignored by all religions. Religious leaders in most parts of the world are also culpable for being so happy to give their blessing to wars entered into by the government, no matter how wrongly.

Equally, those religious leaders that have been actively involved in promoting terrorism in recent decades are also culpable. It is high time we all got wise to the charlatans who profit by religion.

Quality of life

As the quotation that opens this chapter reminds us, quality of life should be our foremost aim. To this end every effort should be made to provide people everywhere with an adequate diet and clean water.

A penalty for our developing language is that there is a need for years of schooling to teach it, along with other basics such as arithmetic, literature and some appreciation of the arts and the sciences. Every child should be given this opportunity and every effort should be made to streamline a much too drawn out education system so that it will be more easily adapted for children everywhere.

Conclusion

The overpopulation issue is obviously the most urgent as the others depend a great deal upon it. As it will take a century or two to reduce our population to more manageable and decently sustainable levels, however, the energy crisis and pollution and resource depletion issues need urgent and maximum attention.

The issues of famine and disease for about half the world's population also deserve no less attention.

That attention should be distracted by needless wars and conflicts as little as possible.

10. Key Policy Objectives

References

Clark, G. *In Fear of China.* Lansdown Press, Melbourne, 1972.

Mohr GA, *The Doomsday Calculation,* Xlibris, Sydney (2014).

Mohr GA, *The Pretentious Persuaders, A Brief History & Science of Mass Persuasion,* 2nd edn, Horizon Publishing Group, Sydney (2014b).

Mohr GA, *Elementary Thinking for the 21st Century,* Xlibris, Sydney (2014c).

Mohr GA, Fear E, *The Brainwashed: From Consumer Zombies to Islamism and Jihad,* Inspiring Publishers, Canberra (2016).

Mohr GA, Mohr PE, Mohr RS, *The Population Explosion: The Problems, Solutions, and Prediction,* Amazon-Kindle (2018).

Sweezy PM, *The Theory of Capitalist Development,* Dennis Dobson, London (1946).

10. Key Policy Objectives

Chapter 11

CONCLUSIONS

> *Protectionism is the institutionalization of economic failure.*
> Edward Heath, British conservative PM, 1970 – 74.
>
> *The seeming uselessness of many economists has been on show recently as more of them have their two bob's worth about tax reform.*
> Judith Sloan, contributing economics editor,
> 'Are economists useful? A question to tax the brain.'
> *The Weekend Australian,* Nov. 21-22, 2015.

Basic economics

Chapter 1 discussed various aspects of business finance, the business sector having, of course, a strong relationship, and a considerable effect upon, a nation's economy.

Chapter 2 discussed International Economics, or Macroeconomics, whilst Chapter 3 discussed Microeconomics, or 'national economics'.

These first three chapters provide a concise introduction to modern economic theories and practices.

They also discuss a few 'economic errors', for example:
(a) That a commodity-dependent economy such as that of Australia should peg its exchange rate.
(b) To prevent the rapid decline in Australia's manufacturing industries in the last decade, as well as the total destruction of its car industry, there should have been at least some modest level of tariff protection.

11. CONCLUSIONS

Economic modelling

Chapter 4 discussed Laurence Klein's 'time-stepping' model of the USA economy from 1921 to 1941. This shows how the various variables in a national economy such as investment, government spending, and taxes affect its overall performance.

With the same parameters, but different 'weighting' of them, any national economy can, of course, be modeled.

Chapter 5 details Jack Vernon's *Liquid Money Supply* (LMS) and *Interest Sensitive Expenditure* (ISE) curves, using the equations for these to prove that *increasing official/government interest rates increases inflation* (usually), and a chart of the fluctuations of the US federal reserve cash rate and US inflation rates from 1954 to 2019 is given as an example of this.

Chapter 6 discussed Input-Output Analysis, which provides a matrix (equation) model of the transactions between businesses. Optimizing IOA problems was also discussed, along with application of constraints to IOA models. Then the Finite Element Method is applied to link two small IOA models.

Chapter 7 discussed the traditional law of supply and demand in which the demand curve goes 'down', this applying to commodities such as food etc., then discussing an alternative 'inverse' law of supply and demand which applies to manufactured products.

Chapter 8 discussed the important issue of globalization, the importance of which has recently been emphasized by a 'tariff war' between the USA and China.

Chapter 9 discussed some key current issues, including:
- The 'energy crisis' and global warming.
- Resource depletion and pollution.
- High levels of government debt in many countries.
- Globalization of markets.
- The high costs of combating global terrorism.
- China's rapid rise.

Finally, Chapter 10 discussed some of the key issues that governments should now be trying to address, whether by economic, diplomatic or other means.

Appendix

Introduction to BASIC

A.1. A brief history of BASIC

BASIC was developed by Kemeny and Kurtz at Dartmouth College (New Hampshire) in the early 1960s and was much used on minicomputers (which typically had 16 terminals, each being allowed 16 kb of RAM, the amount required by the then versions of BASIC) in the 1970s.

In 1975 the first microcomputer was sold, a clumsy box + switches affair with storage of only 256 bytes. In the same year Tiny BASIC, consisting of just 20 pages of code, was written and many versions of this quickly appeared and, also in 1975, Gates and Allen launched Microsoft Corporation with their version, this being marketed with the Altair microcomputer.

A flood of microcomputers with as little as 16 kb of RAM then appeared, the Apple, the Commodore 64, the Spectravideo, the HP85 and many others, all having their own version of BASIC.

In the early 1980s IBM quit their near monopoly of the electric ('golfball') typewriter market, switching to production of *PCs* with about a MB of RAM. Now there was a flood of PCs: Apple, IBM, ICL, NEC, Olivetti etc., as well as many IBM 'clones.'

On the IBM BASICJ, BASICA and GW ('Gee Whiz') BASIC appeared. All used about 64 kb of RAM and the latter is quite powerful. With the advent of a MB of RAM or more Chris Cochran and American Planning Corp's MegaBasic appeared to make full use of it.

Appendix

From Microsoft QBASIC, using a rudimentary GUI (graphic user interface), followed and was shipped with DOS 5 whilst Quick BASIC, the first fully compiled BASIC appeared around the same time, and Visual Basic (VB) for Windows shortly thereafter, this having compilation as an option.

VB4 was still somewhat clumsy to use, but VB5 is very user friendly. VB5 is quick, but not as quick as the original computer language, FORTRAN, or the later C++. There are still reminders of its predecessors, for example the QBColor( ) function.

VB6 and VB7 or VB.NET, however, are about as quick as C++ when compiled so that BASIC is finally competitive speedwise.

The original BASIC feature of having a command interpreter allows programs to run on an almost 'line by line basis without full compilation so you don't type the whole program in, compile and receive a long list of cryptic error messages which don't even tell you where the program stopped. Instead mistyped lines produce an immediate error as you type them.

When you do run the program, therefore, there will be only one error message at a time, telling you when the program stopped and you go to that line and correct the error, and thus work your way through what should be only a few errors.

QBASIC, the version of BASIC used in most of the coding given in this book, can be downloaded free from the internet, as can QuickBASIC, a later version which includes a compiler.

In versions of Windows such as Windows XP and Vista, QBASIC must be run in Command Prompt mode.

In later versions of Windows from Windows 7 to Windows 10, QB4.exe can be obtained in 32-bit and 64-bit versions from www.QB64.org by clicking DOWNLOAD under 'QB64 v1.3 out now!' and on the page that then appears, choosing to download either of the zip files: qb64_1.3_win_x64.7z (64 bit) or qb64_1.3_win_x86.7z (32 bit), and also help_1.3.zip.

The qb64 programs convert the QBASIC code to executable C++ with the output from PRINT commands displayed in a separate window.

[QBASIC programs can also be run via a free program which uses a 'DOS box', but this is confusing to use.]

APPENDIX

A.2. Introduction to BASIC programming

BASIC commands

The most elementary BASIC commands are:

    RUN - to run a program
    SAVE - to store a program
    ENTER - to add lines
    REN - to renumber program lines (with default 'gaps' of 10)
    LIST - to list the program (on screen)
    BYE - to leave BASIC

Arithmetic operations

The following program determines the square toot of a number using Newton's method in which the root is given by iterating the recursion relation

$$x_{new} = (x_{old} + num/x_{old})/2$$

where num = number for which the square root is required

    x_{old} = initial estimate of the square root

Then, using a tolerance number TOL as a termination criterion the program is:

```
10 Rem SQRT using Newton's method
20 INPUT "Input, xold, num,tol", XOLD, NUM, TOL
30 XNEW = 0.5*(XOLD+NUN/XOLD)
40 DIFF = ABS9XNEW-XOLD)
50 IF DIFF<TOL THEN GOTO 80
60 XOLD = XNEW
70 GOTO 30
80 PRINT "SQRT =", NEW
```

and to test the program typical input is 1,4,0.001 to obtain Ö4 = 2.

Note that ABS( ) is a library function for the absolute value and that in some versions of BASIC a final line, 90 END is required (and in VB a first line Sub MYPROG( ) is needed to declare a subroutine).

In early versions of BASIC line numbers were necessary and in very early versions of BASIC variable names were restricted to two a single alphabetic character plus a single optional digit.

APPENDIX

In QBASIC (and VB) line numbers are not necessary and variable names can be many characters but statements are upper case (converted thus if typed otherwise). Then when computation is redirected by a GOTO (or THEN GOTO, for which only half the statement is actually required) statement the target line must have a *label* (e.g. LAB1:) which is given in the GOTO statement. Thus the foregoing example can be written more briefly as

```
INPUT xold, num, tol
LAB1: xnew = (xold + num/xold)/2 : diff = ABS(xnew-xold)
IF diff<tol GOTO LAB2
xold = xnew: GOTO LAB1
LAB2:PRINT xnew
```

where a semicolon is used as a *statement separator*. The author, however, generally uses line numbers throughout his programs, one reason being that, having put many BASIC programs in books, they are very handy in this situation to help describe the program (i.e. "lines 110 - 160 do - - - ').

Strings

Ease of string handling is one of the traditional advantages of BASIC. The following program reads three names (given in the DATA statements at the end) and prints them (on screen) with three spaces between. It then prints an integer and a real number using PRINT USING to *format* these.

```
10 READ a$, b$, c$
20 x$ = SPACES$(3)
30 PRINT A$;x$;b$;x$;c$
40 P$="#####" : Q$ = "#####.##"
50 n = 2 : c = 14/3
60 PRINT USING P$ ; n ; : PRINT USING Q$;c
70 DATA 'Bob", "Jim", "Ted"
```

Note that a ; follows the 'n' of the first PRINT USING statement to print both numbers on the same line, otherwise the second number will appear on a second line.

Here in line 40 P$ is in *integer* format and Q$ is in *real number* format. Strictly variables should be *declared* at the start of the program as *integer, real, double precision* etc.

Arrays and Loops

The following *database* program dimensions (i.e declares their size) *arrays* and then uses a *loop* (on i) to read some names and ages and print them out, right justifying the names using the LEN function.

```
DIM names$(10),num(10)
FOR i = 1 to 3
READ names$(i), num(i)
j = LEN(names(i)) : x$ = SPACE$( j )
PRINT x$;names$(i),num(i) : NEXT
DATA "Jane" , 25
DATA "June" , 35
DATA "Caroline" , 15
```

Functions

Finally we give a simple example of a user defined function to calculate the square of a number. Note the way the variable X is passed to the function as an *argument* and the function result is returned as R.

```
10 DECLARE FUNCTION SQ(Z)
20 Z=2
30 Y = SQ(Z)
40 PRINT Z
100 FUNCTION SQ(Z)
110 Z=Z*Z
END FUNCTION
```

Note that QBASIC automatically stores the function as a *subroutine* in a separate *workspace* accessed via the VIEW menu from the menu bar (at the top of the screen).

Standard functions

Standard arithmetic, mathematical and string functions used in BASIC include

INT( ) - gives the integer (truncated) value of a number
ABS( ) - gives absolute value of a number (unsigned)
RND(x) - gives a random number [x <0 gives same number, x> 0 (or x not given) gives the next number in the sequence, = 0 gives the last number]
SQR( ) - gives square root

APPENDIX

SIN( ) - gives SIN( ) of an angle in radians
LEN(A$) - see example program in "Arrays and loops" earlier in this section
CHR$(n) - gives the ASCII character corresponding to integer n
(e.g. n = 65 gives A)

Subroutines

The simplest way of forming subroutines is using the GOSUB command to move to program segments appended after the END statement

```
10 PRINT "main"
20 GOSUB 50
30 PRINT "main"
40 END
50 PRINT "sub"
60 RETURN
```

Alternatively subroutines are stored as separate programs and called by a main program. The following program is called MAIN. It has a subroutine 'datin' which is called and numbers passed to it, omitting one number so that it prints as zero when the number list is printed while in the subroutine.

```
DECLARE SUB datin (N, M)
REM MAIN
DIM X(10), Y(10)
COMMON SHARED Y()
X(1) = 5: Y(2) = 3: N = 10: M = 10
datin N, M
PRINT "main", X(1), Y(2), N, M
END

SUB datin (N, M)
DIM X(10)
PRINT "sub", X(1), Y(2), N, M
END SUB
```

Here the argument list passes N, M to the subroutine and the COMMON SHARED statement allows listed variables to be accessed by all other subroutines. As the array X() is not included in the shared statement, X(1) will print from the subroutine as zero.

Appendix

Data files

Here we give a examples of a data files (as distinct from program files) using the following program.

```
OPEN "c:\basic\temdat" FOR OUTPUT AS #7
OPEN "c:\basic\gmdata" FOR RANDOM AS #8 LEN = 100
x = 2: y = 3
PUT #8, 1, x :PUT #8, 2, y
WRITE #7, x, y
CLOSE #7
OPEN "c:\basic\temdat" FOR INPUT AS #7
GET #8, 2, z : PRINT z
INPUT #7, z : PRINT z
```

Here two files are used for *sequential* access and *direct* or *random* access, in the second case overestimating the *record* length and reading back only the second number written to it.

As another example the following code accesses a .DBF file in which a list of names, account numbers, balances and dates is stored:

```
OPEN "\gmwork\accs.dbf" FOR INPUT AS #8
ON ERROR GOTO pend
PRINT "Start"
FOR i = 1 TO 4: INPUT #8, a$
PRINT a$: PRINT: NEXT
pend: PRINT "end"
END
```

The file had data for only three people and was set up using Lotus Approach but .DBF files are used by other programs such as Q&A and Sortit. The ERROR statement is to end the program without error message interruption when end of file (EOF) is encountered. As should be expected, the recovered data includes headings and is printed without formatting. In this instance the account number heading was 'a/c #' which did disturb reading of the headings slightly.

APPENDIX

Searching and comparing data

The following code is a very simple example of comparing data, in this case string data. In conjunction with search, therefore, such comparisons can be used to locate specific data.

```
10 a$ = "jim" : b$ = "jim"
30 IF a$ = b$ THEN PRINT "OK"
40 b$="ted"
50 IF a$ = b$ THEN PRINT "OK" ELSE PRINT "NO"
```

In the previous example program such comparisons might be used to extract negative numbers (perhaps corresponding to negative account balances) and the associated personal details from a file.

A.3. Sorting routines

The simplest type of sort is a *bubble sort* in which we successively pass down through the numbers, interchanging pairs of numbers when the second exceeds the first. Eventually the numbers fall into descending order but it takes over 2000 calculations to sort 100 short integer numbers.

More efficient is *search sorting* which seeks out the maximum number of those remaining to be sorted and places this at the top of these. This takes over 400 calculations for the 100 number sort.

More efficient are *hybrid* sorting routines which combine the two approaches and sometimes use *recursion* (i.e., the subroutine calls itself) and take only about 250 calculations for the 100 number sort.

A program using the *Quick Sort* method is given below, this using recursion. It lives up to its name and takes about 180 calculations for the 100 number test.

```
DIM H, L, ii AS LONG
DECLARE SUB quicksort (a(), L, H)
DECLARE SUB partition (L, H, ii, a())
DIM a(101)
FOR i = 1 TO 100: VALUE = RND(.5) * 100: a(i) = INT(VALUE):
NEXT
calcs = 0
CALL quicksort(a(), 1, 100)
FOR i = 1 TO 100: PRINT a(i); : NEXT
PRINT "Calcs = ", calcs
```

```
SUB partition (L, H, ii, a())
SHARED calcs: DIM i, j AS LONG
piv = a(L): i = L: j = H + 1
REM Choose pivot as first element in range
DO
  DO
   i = i + 1: REM From start look for larger # (if there is)
   LOOP UNTIL a(i) > piv OR i >= H
  DO
   j = j - 1: REM From end look for smaller # (if there is)
   LOOP UNTIL a(j) < piv OR j <= L
         REM If they haven't crossed swap them
  IF i < j THEN
    temp = a(i): a(i) = a(j): a(j) = temp: calcs = calcs + 1
  END IF
LOOP UNTIL j <= i: REM Swap pivot with the split in the array
a(L) = a(j): a(j) = piv: calcs = calcs + 1
ii = j: REM Return index of # in correct location for next 'split sort'
END SUB

SUB quicksort (a(), L, H)
REM If the range is valid then sort
IF L < H THEN
REM Split the array & return index of the item in the correct location
CALL partition(L, H, ii, a())
REM Sort the lower portion
CALL quicksort(a(), L, ii - 1)
REM Sort the upper portion
CALL quicksort(a(), ii + 1, H)
END IF
END SUB
```

Finally note that it is sometimes necessary, and generally a wise precaution, to declare variable types as *integer, real* (the default), or *double precision* using the DEFINT, DEFSNG, DEFDBL statements. Alternatively this can be done globally as the first line of a program using:

DefSng A-H, O-Z: DefInt I-N

to reserve I-N for integers, as is the default in FORTRAN, the original programming language.

APPENDIX

A.4. Visual BASIC (VB)

Visual basic programs usually begin with a form, Form1, for which the coding:

Private Sub Form-Load( )

End Sub

is automatically added when VB starts the new program with Form1.

Then one can add BASIC coding, to obtain, for example:

Private Sub Form-Load( )
Show
x = 2
y = 3
z = x + y
Print "z =", z
End Sub

Here the command Show is necessary to print on the form. Alternatively, one can have VB add a coding Module to contain the commands of one's program. This will take the form:

Sub main( )
y = 2
x = 3
z = x+ y
Form1.Print "z = ", z
End Sub

and to run this include the command line

Call main

in the coding for Form1.

Regrettably, perhaps, VB does not have DATA statements, so that data must be read from a separate file, though for just a few values of variables, of course, these can be 'declared' as above.

APPENDIX

As a VB example, the following coding plots simple vibrations.

The coding for Form1, which has a Command button added to it that is pressed to start the program, is

```
Private Sub Command2_Click()
Call main
End Sub

Private Sub Form_Load()

End Sub
```

The coding in the program module for the vibration plotting is:

```
Public output As Object
Sub main()
Rem Time stepping vibration program
Set output = Form1
output.FontSize = 20
output.Print "             VIBRATION PLOT"
output.Line (0, 0)-(0, 0): output.DrawWidth = 5
A1 = 0: B1 = 0: A2 = 0: B2 = 0: XL = 0: SL = 0: F = 40
output.Line (0, 0)-(0, 8000): output.Line (0, 4000)-(8000, 4000)
For T = 0 To 2.5 Step 0.1
S = 0: If T <= 0.5 Then S = 1
A3 = 1.5 * A2 + B2 / 2 - A1: B3 = S + A2 / 2 + B2 - B1: X = 120 * T
Z = 100 - 20 * SL: Y = 100 - 20 * S: X = F * X: Z = F * Z: Y = F * Y
output.Line (XL, Z)-(X, Y)
Z = 100 - 20 * B2: Y = 100 - 20 * B3: Z = F * Z: Y = F * Y
output.Line (XL, Z)-(X, Y)
Z = 100 - 20 * A2: Y = 100 - 20 * A3: Z = F * Z: Y = F * Y
output.Line (XL, Z)-(X, Y)
A1 = A2: B1 = B2: A2 = A3: B2 = B3
XL = X: SL = S: Next
End Sub
```

After running the program the resulting plotting on Form 1 comes out as follows, showing the a small initial disturbance, along with the vibration of two parameters which, for example, might be the movement at two levels of a building subjected to an earthquake.

APPENDIX

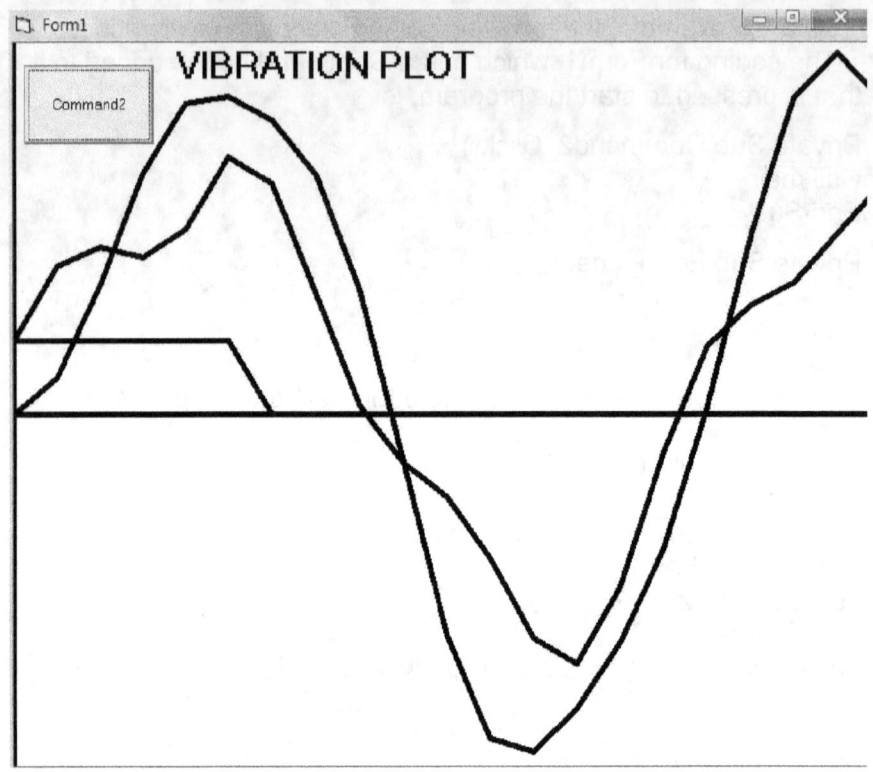

References

Brown S, *Visual Basic in Record Time,* Sybex, Alameda CA 1998.

Capron HL, Williams BK, *Computers and Data Processing*, Benjamin Cummings, Menlo Park CA, 1982.

Cochran C, *MegaBasic Users Manual*, American Planning Corp., Alexandria VA 1984.,

Fox D, *Pure Visual Basic*, Sams 1999.

Kreitzberg CB, Scheidman B, *The Elements of FORTRAN Style,* HBJ, NY, 1972.

Lien DA, *The BASIC Handbook,* 3rd edn, Microtech, Dubai, UAE, 1989.

Appendix

Perry G, *Introduction to Computer Programming*, SAMS, New York, 2001.

Price WT, *Fundamentals of Computers and Data Processing with Basic*, Holt, Rinehard and Winston, New York NY, 1983.

Time-Life (eds), *Computer Languages*, Time-Life Inc. 1986.

MS GW-BASIC User's Guide and User's Reference, MS Corp., 1987.

Appendix

ECONOMICS: A CONCISE INTRODUCTION

The book begins with three comprehensive chapters on:
> Business Finance.
> International Economics (macroeconomics).
> Microeconomics (national economics).

Next come chapters on economic models and methodologies that are new, or not found in most books on economics:
> Time stepping models of national economies.
> The Liquid Money Supply and Interest Sensitive Expenditure curves, using the equations for these to show that increasing official interest rates increase inflation, as intuition suggests.
> Input-output analysis, a matrix model of the business sector.
> An 'inverted' supply and demand model for manufactured products (the original model applying to commodities).
> Three chapters on globalization and other key current issues.

G. A. Mohr did his PhD at Churchill College, Cambridge.
He published circa 60 journal papers and 40+ books, including:
A Microcomputer Introduction to the Finite Element Method
Finite Elements for Solids, Fluids, and Optimization
The Pretentious Persuaders, A Brief History & Science of Mass Persuasion
Curing Cancer & Heart Disease;   The Variant Virus
The Doomsday Calculation, The End Of The Human Race
Heart Disease, Cancer, & Ageing: Proven Neutraceutical & Lifestyle Solutions
2045: A Remote Town Survives Global Holocaust
The History & Psychology of Human Conflict;   The War of the Sexes
Elementary Thinking for the 21st Century
The 8-Week+ Program to Reverse Cardiovascular Disease
The Scientific MBA;   Mohr's Law of Hierarchies
The DIY Cardiovascular Cure;   Combating Cancer
New Ideas for the 21st Century
Also with R.S. Mohr/Richard Sinclair & P.E. Mohr/Edwin Fear:
The Evolving Universe: Relativity, Redshift and Life from Space
World Religions: The History, Psychology, Issues & Truth
World War 3, When & How Will It End?
The Brainwashed, From Consumer Zombies to Islamic Jihad
Human Intelligence, Learning & Behaviour
New Theories of The Universe, Evolution, and Relativity
The Psychology of Hope;   The Population Explosion
Brainwashed Zombies: Religious, Political & Consumer Persuasion
Human Conflict: An Attitudinal Psychology Model

www.ingramcontent.com/pod-product-compliance
Lightning Source LLC
Chambersburg PA
CBHW070625220526
45466CB00001B/100